MW01706439

CAVENDISH GARDENS
CANADIAN PRACTICAL GUIDES

HERB GARDENS

CAVENDISH GARDENS
CANADIAN PRACTICAL GUIDES

HERB GARDENS

RICHARD ROSENFELD

CAVENDISH BOOKS
VANCOUVER

A DK PUBLISHING BOOK
www.dk.com

PROJECT EDITOR Cangy Venables
ART EDITOR Margherita Gianni

SERIES EDITOR Pamela Brown
SERIES ART EDITOR Stephen Josland
US EDITOR Ray Rogers

MANAGING EDITOR Louise Abbott
MANAGING ART EDITOR Lee Griffiths

DTP DESIGNER Matthew Greenfield

PRODUCTION MANAGER Patricia Harrington

First Canadian Edition, 1999
2 4 6 8 10 9 7 5 3

Published in Canada by
Cavendish Books Inc., Unit 23, 1610 Derwent Way, Delta, BC V3M 6W1
www.gardenbooks.com

Published in Great Britain by Dorling Kindersley Limited.

A CIP record for this book is available from the National Library, Ottawa

ISBN 1 55289 003 1

Reproduced by Colourscan, Singapore
Printed and bound by Star Standard Industries, Singapore

CONTENTS

HERBS IN THE GARDEN

WHAT IS AN HERB?

THE WORD "HERB" has been used for centuries to describe plants with medicinal, culinary, and aromatic properties, many linked with spiritual well-being and sacred rites. No working kitchen garden was complete without a scattering of favorites such as parsley and thyme, and the simplicity of cottage-style herbs is still valued in informal plantings. But it is the formal, patterned herb gardens of the past that are popular today – features that are not only useful but also rich with historical associations and of lasting ornamental value.

HOW HERB GARDENS DEVELOPED

The making of special gardens in which herbs are grown and displayed has a long history. Obviously, such gardens gathered useful plants together for convenience, but there is much more of a tradition of making decorative features out of these plantings than for vegetables.

From the earliest records, herbs have been associated with religion. In ancient Persia, the enclosed garden filled with scented and healing plants provided a sanctuary or "paradise" for meditation. Stylistically, European monastic gardens followed the Eastern tradition – peaceful retreats sheltered from the outside world, in which narrow pathways divided small beds that were not just decorative, but practical: powerful medicinal herbs could be grown separately, with no likelihood of confusion when gathered by novices.

RESTFUL FORMALITY
In this scene from an ancient Eastern garden, where plants each had their own separate areas, the origins of the formal garden style with patterned, edged beds can be seen.

◀ HERBS AS GARDEN PLANTS
Herbs can be used in mixed plantings (here, sage with apples, roses, and geraniums), but special herb gardens have great appeal.

Herb Gardens for Study

The study of plants and their medicinal uses spread from religious to scholarly institutions, who adopted the form of the patterned herb garden with herbs in discrete beds as a way of cultivating and displaying plants for ease of study by botanists, doctors, and artists. The first of these "physic gardens" recorded in detail was created in Italy at the University of Padua in 1545, followed by others at Leyden, Holland, in 1587 and Oxford in 1621. By the end of the 17th century, there were physic gardens throughout Europe.

As colonial explorers and plant hunters brought back different species, more and more herbs from other cultures were added to the gardens' ever-expanding collections. Settlers took plants and gardening traditions with them, too: the first botanical garden in North America was created near Philadelphia in 1728, and traditional European-style herb gardens can still be seen in the US, Canada, Australia, New Zealand, and South Africa.

▲ EARLY EASTERN REPRESENTATION
This illustration from an early Arabic text shows an emphasis on botanical detail, marking a new appreciation of herbs as garden plants.

▼ GARDEN OF PRIVACY
This gorgeously patterned, 17th-century walled garden has walkways between the beds.

Herbs in Private Gardens

Meanwhile, however, cottage gardeners continued to grow herbs informally among ornamental plants much as they always had, both for their decorative qualities and to add to the cooking pot. But the formal, well-tended herb gardens of the institutions had enormous snob appeal for rich, private landowners, being just the sort of labor-intensive feature that displayed obvious wealth and, as a bonus, reflected the owner's scholarly and aesthetic appreciation of "nature." Soon herbs, formerly humble plants of the kitchen garden, were being grown prominently in elaborate parterres, potagers, and knot gardens in palaces, stately homes, and country seats.

> Today, herb gardening is undergoing a great revival

Herb Gardening Today

The great revival of interest in herb gardening today combines elements from the scholarly, grand, and cottage traditions. In the East, herb growing has largely remained functional, for medicinal purposes; in their own gardens, the Chinese and Japanese do not regard herbs as ornamentals. But in the West, it is their decorative appeal and culinary uses that are more appreciated, and herbs can be seen growing everywhere from windowsills to herbaceous borders, used simply as ornamental plants or, in today's smaller gardens, in greatly scaled-down versions of the more formal, patterned beds. There are specialized nurseries where you might find 18 varieties of basil and 50 lavenders; in the wake of such popularity, even the more obscure herbs, such as skirret and fleabane, are making a comeback.

MODERN HERB GARDEN
Modern herb gardens often echo the past, as with this decorative sundial centerpiece.

WHY GROW HERBS?

HERBS ARE VERSATILE PLANTS. They will grow happily in most environments, they suit small gardens well, and they can be used in all sorts of ways. You may grow them for cooking or simple herbal remedies, for use in crafts and hobbies, for making potpourris and sachets for scenting clothes and bedlinen, and even for dyeing. Alternatively, you could design an herb garden simply to provide a peaceful retreat, filled with soft colors and soothing aromas.

PLANTING WITH HERBS

The attraction of herbs lies to a large extent in their uses, historical associations, and fragrance. The sheer number of different herbs now available, however, makes them increasingly valuable as ornamental plants. Flowers can be vivid – the red of bee balm and the oranges and yellows of pot marigolds, for example – and foliage attractive: the silver-gray of lavender, the dusky tones of purple sage, and the bright splash of golden marjoram.

Herbs lend themselves to both formal and informal use. Bear in mind that formal patterns need to be kept in order; plants must be chosen carefully and kept neat and dense with regular care and clipping. But many herbs are large, wild plants with a naturally loose, spreading habit; these can be allowed to grow and self-seed at will for a more informal effect.

FORMAL HERB FEATURE
This purely decorative feature uses different colored gravels to enhance a living pattern made of clipped herb plants.

HERBS IN POTS
Herbs with tough, wiry stems that grow naturally in poor or hot, dry soil are perfect for pots. Here (from left) *bay, santolina, rosemary, and thymes form an attractive, aromatic group. Softer-stemmed plants such as parsley (second from left) can be pot-grown but need regular watering.*

Growing Herbs for Use

Today, most gardeners grow herbs to pick chiefly for their culinary uses (*see pp.12–13*); for this, a specially made herb garden or bed is ideal, keeping all the plants needed together and readily accessible. Many herbs grow well in containers (*pp.46–51*); these may be placed on steps, windowsills, or conveniently by the kitchen door. Regular harvesting of the herbs helps keep them in check, preventing them from swamping their neighbors or spoiling a design.

> Regular harvesting of herbs helps keep them shapely and in check

The medicinal purposes of herbs should be treated with respect and caution, but many can be grown in small herb gardens for occasional use in simple, therapeutic ways (*see pp.16–17*), such as in teas and infusions. Herbs grown for crafts and hobbies (*see pp.18–20*) may need to be grown in greater quantity, so you should plan to allocate more room for them, maybe giving individual plants or types of plants beds of their own.

▲ KITCHEN HERB GARDEN
Narrow beds of culinary herbs no more than 3ft/1m across, with paths alongside, make access for tending and harvesting easy.

▼ HERBS IN INFORMAL PLANTINGS
Untamed herbs grown in the ornamental border create a lovely, naturalistic effect, with the added attraction of encouraging wildlife.

CULINARY HERBS

CULINARY HERBS, mostly easy to grow, can enhance the flavor of any dish. Whatever size your garden, there will be room to generate plenty of wonderful tastes. The range of kitchen herbs includes shrubs, perennials, and annuals that may be creeping, clump-forming, towering, or even climbing in habit; enough, in a small garden, to create a completely edible landscape.

A KITCHEN HERB GARDEN

An herb garden designed with healing plants to provide a quiet retreat might well be best situated in an out-of-the-way part of the garden, but if you plan to use the herbs as a kitchen resource, it's more practical either to incorporate them into the kitchen garden, if you have one, or to grow them together near the house. Here, your herb bed probably will be on show by a door or visible from windows, so it makes sense to design it as an attractive feature that will not look bare and gloomy in winter. Hard landscaping materials can be a real bonus: a checkerboard design (*see pp.28–32*) set into a patio, for example, has year-round structural appeal, as do groups of interesting containers (*see pp.34–39*) or brick-patterned beds (*see pp.46–51*). But there are shrubby, evergreen kitchen herbs that can add structure to a planting: rosemary, sages, and thymes, for example (though they do look a little scruffy after a cold winter). For elegant good looks and usefulness year-round, few plants beat a carefully shaped bay tree; not cheap to buy, but a lasting investment. If you don't mind losing the outlines of your beds in winter, there are lots of herbaceous culinary herbs that make beautiful edging: rows of chives allowed to flower, for example, or emerald ribbons of curly parsley.

HERBS IN THE BORDER
Culinary herbs that you do not use often can be scattered among plantings of ornamentals: here, feathery dill and large-leaved lovage add height with foxgloves, while golden marjoram weaves through santolina. Grow them in groups or drifts so that any harvesting does not spoil the planting.

Flavors and Foliage

Your choice of herbs to fill kitchen beds will probably be guided more by their flavors (*see p.14*) than by looks, and you may find that foliage plants with relatively small flowers predominate. With some herbs, too, such as arugula and basil, flowerheads need removing regularly if the leaves are to retain their flavor (this can be surprisingly time-consuming). But even using foliage it is possible to ring color changes – with, for example, silver sage or purple-leaved basil. You could also allot a little space to some herbs with edible flowers; a small tepee of stakes covered with climbing nasturtiums would make a striking centerpiece for a symmetrical culinary herb garden.

> Remove flowerheads from basil and arugula to intensify the flavor

▲ A FEAST OF FOLIAGE
Nasturtiums and pot marigolds, which can be used in salads, will brighten up a group of leafy kitchen herbs. Here, mints grown in pots to restrain them can be moved to fill gaps.

▼ FLOWERING FREELY
Grow plenty of chives (here with fennel and Good King Henry) so that you can allow some to develop their drumstick flowerheads.

Growing Herbs for the Kitchen

If you are used to cooking with herbs, you will probably have some ideas about what you want to grow in a culinary herb garden. But if you are a new cook (and particularly if you are a new gardener, too), it's not easy to know which will be the most useful herbs, how many plants you should buy, and – with so many different types to choose from – which are actually the culinary herbs and which are the more ornamental, less flavorsome varieties.

How Much Space?

You can make a kitchen herb "survival kit" in a container no larger than a shoebox (*see below*), but you must be prepared to tend, water, trim, and even replace plants frequently: many different plants packed together like this will not thrive for long, although they do make a more lasting resource than the small pots of living herbs available at supermarkets. With a small herb garden, you can grow a whole range of herbs happily together, provided that you take measures to restrain inveterate spreaders such as mints and marjorams. Don't waste space, either, in a small herb garden on a lot of large plants that you will use only rarely; they can be accommodated instead in a border, if attractive, or in a corner of a vegetable plot.

Which Herbs to Choose?

Herbs are so popular these days that it is now usual to see herb plants labeled with common names at garden centers, so you don't need to know their Latin names, but, even so, you need to choose carefully – eau-de-cologne mint may be a prettier plant than common mint, but it will give new potatoes a very peculiar flavor.

Faced with a wide range of herb plants attractively displayed, it's tempting to fill a a basket with a dozen small specimens, all

MINI KITCHEN GARDEN
A windowsill could accommodate this wire basket, lined with moss and pierced plastic and filled with soil mix, but you must tend and water the plants regularly. Always plant mints in their pots to prevent them from overwhelming other plants. At the end of the summer, it is best to plant all the hardy herbs into the garden.

BIG DECISIONS
If space is limited, be ruthless and reserve your herb garden for kitchen favorites (below). *Borage* (left) *may be pretty, but you probably won't use it that often: a large plant, it is better sited where there is more room for it.*

of different kinds. However, not only will this make your herb garden look spotty, but it will take an age for them to grow large enough to be useful: one recipe calling for a handful of chervil could demolish an entire plant. Three or four plants each of the true kitchen standbys soon make attractive and productive clumps.

> Always grow twice as much parsley as you think you need

How Many Plants?

With some herb flavors, less is definitely more, but fresh, leafy summer herbs such as cilantro are best by the bunchful. As a general rule, and perhaps a frustrating one for gardeners less confident of their skills, the more robust and long-lived the plant, the less you need to use of it. A single rosemary bush, for example, needs virtually no looking after and can supply several kitchens with sprigs for years, but if your dishes regularly call for great handfuls of parsley and basil, bought plants will not last, and you will need to consider growing your own plants from seed (*see p.56*), sowing not just once but several times during the spring and summer to keep plants coming.

CLASSIC COMBINATIONS

Standby herbs for different dishes include:

Fish Bay, chervil, dill, fennel, lovage, parsley, sorrel, sweet cicely, winter savory.

Beef Bay, rosemary, tarragon, thyme.

Chicken Chervil, chives, cilantro, fennel, parsley, tarragon.

Pork Basil, cilantro, fennel, pot marigold, marjoram, parsley, sorrel, thyme.

Lamb Cilantro, oregano, parsley, rosemary.

Eggs Basil, chervil, chives, cilantro, dill, fennel, summer savory, sorrel, tarragon, thyme.

Medicinal Herbs

PLANTS WERE THE FIRST MEDICINES available and have played an important role in our well-being ever since. When different cultures started recording knowledge they had gained, the healing potential of herbs was a key subject. Nearly 1,000 years before the West even had a printing press, the Chinese produced their *Canon*, listing over 800 medicinal herbs and their uses.

Herbs with Healing Powers

In any country, it takes years of training to become a qualified herbalist, but, in cultures where herbal medicine is not now mainstream, we have largely forgotten that there was a time when everyone would instinctively seek out certain plants as simple remedies. Today, we are far more likely to reach for the medicine cabinet for relief from pain or discomfort, although many undoubtedly effective folk remedies do persist – applying an aloe to a burn, for example. Western medical science has, however, long acknowledged a debt to the herbal tradition – while our forebears chewed willow bark to alleviate headaches, we might now take aspirin, whose active ingredient, salicylic acid, was first isolated

Modern medical science has long acknowledged its debt to plants

in willow (*Salix*). While it can be interesting to experiment on a small scale with simple, safe remedies for some mild

▶ CLARY SAGE
The Latin name, Salvia, *for this healing herb comes from the word for "safe."*

▼ ESSENCES AND OILS
The benefits of evening-primrose oil are widely recognized.

TWO FOR TEA
Fresh sprigs of mint or chamomile (left) *make soothing teas when steeped in boiling water. Let mint tea cool, adding some honey if desired, for a refreshing summer drink.*

discomforts (*see below*), it is essential not to dabble further into herbal medicine without guidance or the help of an authoritative book. What you can do, however, without preparing or taking any remedy at all, is simply to benefit from the therapeutic effects of making and tending a garden planted with herbs that have healing properties and associations. The attractions of, say, a daily glass of borage infusion might soon begin to pall, but you will gain lasting enjoyment from a herb garden full of pretty plants with relaxing or uplifting aromas: a place to unwind and let tensions ease away. The scents, tactile foliage, quiet orderliness of the beds, and their air of seclusion have made this type of "healing" herb garden increasingly popular; indeed, for many hospitals they are now *de rigueur* as an outdoor sunroom in which convalescent patients can benefit from the restorative power of plants.

SOME SIMPLE REMEDIES	METHOD
Teas: mint to settle the stomach; chamomile or vervain to soothe; lemon balm to uplift.	Immerse 2½oz/75g of fresh herbs (or 1oz/30g of dried) in 2 cups/500ml of near-boiling water.
Infusions: borage and lavender to fight colds; yarrow to relieve congestion; lemon balm to relieve flatulence.	Make as for tea; allow to cool and use as a specific remedy or as an invigorating drink. It is best to make infusions fresh each day.
Ointments: arnica or comfrey to quell bruising; chamomile or St. John's wort to alleviate minor skin conditions.	Heat 2oz/60g of dried herbs in 16oz/500g petroleum jelly over boiling water for about 2 hours. While hot, strain into jar. Allow to cool.
Inhalations: borage and lavender to fight colds; yarrow to relieve congestion.	Add 2 cups/500ml of an infusion (*above*) to a basin of hot water. Inhale steam under a towel.
Bath relaxant or tonic: chamomile or vervain as a relaxant; comfrey, pot marigold, nettle, or yarrow as a restorative tonic.	Fill a muslin bag with fresh or dried herbs. Fasten neck and hang around hot water faucet so that water soaks it. Squeeze juice into bath.

Herbs for the Home

Other traditional uses for herbs are preserved in many crafts and hobbies. Dried, they can be enjoyed in lasting ways around the home – in bowls of potpourri, as garlands and wreaths, and in dried flower arrangements. They can scent pillows, sachets, candles, and writing paper and form the basis for many traditional dyes (*see p.20*). Remember that the more serious you become about your hobby, the more space you will need to allocate to plants.

Potpourris and Wreaths

Easy to make, a potpourri consists of a mixture of dried flowers and scented foliage, sometimes with seedheads and dried bark. Druggists and craft stores stock special fixatives, complete with instructions, which lock in the aromas for longer – powdered orris root and gum benzoin are the most common. You can also buy essential oils to boost or revive scents. Use these frugally, however, since they easily dominate more subtle aromas.

For drying (*see p.58*), herb leaves should be picked early, the moment the dew has evaporated, and flowers as they open. You might choose a theme for a potpourri: an herb-leaf mix, or a flower, lemon, or even wild garden mix. For an herb-leaf potpourri try lemon balm, marjoram, mint, rosemary, sage, and thyme. To a flower mix made bright with bee balm and yarrow, add other scented garden flowers, such as roses and mock orange. For spicy winter scents, try mixing freshly ground cardamom, cloves, coriander, and fennel seed with dried lemon, lime, and orange peel. Cover for 4–6 weeks before using to allow time for the scents to blend and intensify. Another traditional way of displaying herbs is in a wreath. Roll up a rectangle of chicken wire and join the ends to form a ring frame, then weave in

> Pick herbs early in the morning, as soon as the dew is dry

SUMMER SCENTS *Bags of dried lavender are a favorite way of keeping linen fresh, bringing memories of summer scents all year round. This lavender, with its zany bracts, is* Lavandula stoechas, *or French lavender; it needs a sheltered spot.*

fresh thyme, sage, lavender, and rosemary with sphagnum moss. Allow to dry in a warm, airy place. Simple bunches of dried herbs in a basket also look decorative.

More Herb Ideas

For the bedroom, take a few handfuls of potpourri and sew them inside small, decorative covers to put beside pillows. You could even make aromatic sachets to hang in the car. Scented candles can be made by adding dried herbs just before the mold stage. You can also make scented notepaper by scattering layers of dried herbs between the sheets in a box.

Even if you are not the least bit "crafty," herbs can enhance the home. Simple but stylish, fresh bunches of leafy and flowering herbs make lovely table decorations for summer parties and meals, with a home-made look that bought flowers cannot match. A deft touch for a dinner party is to put small bowls of fresh herbs – for example, parsley, basil, and arugula – on the table, so that guests can help themselves.

▲FRAGRANCE IN THE HOME
Many scented plants, including meadowsweet, above, were once used as strewing herbs, scattered on bare floors to cover other, less attractive smells.

▼BOLD AND BEAUTIFUL
For large bowls, make bold potpourris with whole dried flowerheads to avoid the shredded, "nose-bag" look; here, yarrow and pot marigolds contribute to a sunny theme.

WOAD

COMFREY

CONTRASTING COLORS
Yellow-flowered woad has been used to produce a blue color for centuries, while comfrey will yield a sunny yellow dye.

Dyeing with Herbs

Dyeing is tricky but fun, and you need a room where splashes will not be a problem. Note, too, that each batch of dye solution will produce a slightly different color. If dyeing natural wool, you need to scour it first by washing thoroughly or soaking for a few hours to remove any oil. The dye is made in advance; the process usually involves steeping herbs in a bowl of water for eight hours before simmering them for two more. Cool the solution, remove the herbs, add the garment, and simmer again for an hour. Then simmer the garment in a commercial mordant solution that will fix the color, following the instructions for quantities and timing. Different mordants can produce different colors from the same plant (*see below*). When the solution has again cooled, remove the garment with tongs and rinse it until the water is clear.

> The intensity of dye colors depends on the quantity of the herb used

COLORS FROM HERB DYES

HERB	PART USED	MORDANT	COLOR
Agrimony	Flowering tops	Alum	Butter yellow
Comfrey	Whole plant	Alum	Yellow
Chamomile	Flowers	Alum, cream of tartar	Bright yellow
Meadowsweet	Roots	Alum	Black
Nettles	Whole plant	Alum, cream of tartar, pinch of ferrous sulfate	Greenish gray
Nettles	Whole plant	Copper sulfate	Soft gray-green
Parsley	Whole plant	Alum	Cream
Pot marigold	Petals	Alum, cream of tartar	Pale yellow
Safflower	Flowers	Alum	Yellow and tan
St. John's wort	Flowers	Alum	Cream
Sorrel	Whole plant	Alum	Grayish yellow
Sorrel	Roots	Alum	Soft pink
Tansy	Flowering tops	Alum	Mustard yellow
Woad	Leaves	Sodium dithionite, ammonia	Blue

MAKING AN HERB GARDEN

KNOT GARDENS P.23

A SPECIALLY DESIGNED HERB GARDEN is an ideal way to grow and display plants. The projects shown here are all on a small scale and easy to lay out, build, and plant in no more than a weekend, but you can adjust the dimensions to suit your own needs: a builder's supply store should be able to advise on increasing quantities of materials, if necessary. The time taken for the feature to mature might, however, influence your choice: a formal garden that uses plants as edging (*see pp.22–27*) will take a few years to look its best, while paving- or brick-surrounded beds (*see pp.28–39*) will fill out within a season, and a pretty container packed with young plants (*see pp.46–51*) can look splendid almost immediately. There is no "best" time of year to start making an herb garden, although spring provides both clement conditions for working and gives young plants the whole season in which to grow. Similarly, there is no "best" site; although most herbs do prefer a sunny position, you can gather together a selection of plants that thrive in shade. The majority are not fussy about soil, although you might need to improve drainage (*see p.52*), particularly if you want to grow plants native to Mediterranean regions: for these, a specifically made scree or gravel garden (*see pp.40–45*) is ideal.

BRICK WHEEL P.35

SCREE GARDEN P.41

HERB CASCADE P.49

Formal Herb Gardens

COMPACT HERBS ARE IDEALLY SUITED to formal features. Their extensive range of leaf shapes and colors can be used both to create distinct geometric patterns and to fill large squares and loops of clipped low edging. Knot gardens and parterres provide popular design templates, using hedging herbs to create compartments within which any type and number of herbs can be contained. The design may be simple or complex, much of its character derived from the type of plants used and the regularity with which edging is clipped.

A Simple Boxwood-edged Garden

This basic pattern covers an area about 11×11ft/3.3×3.3m and consists of four beds divided by paths. Below the paths and edging, a sheet of landscape fabric suppresses weeds and conserves soil moisture. Allow two days to complete the project.

HEDGING TIPS

- Buy all hedging plants from the same nursery – or grow your own for economy – so they are of a uniform standard.
- Trim boxwood plants in late spring and late summer; never when frost is likely.
- When clipping, a sheet of plastic laid alongside the hedge will collect trimmings.

COMPLETED GARDEN
Allow three to five years for boxwood to mature, during which time regular trimming is essential to perfect its shape.

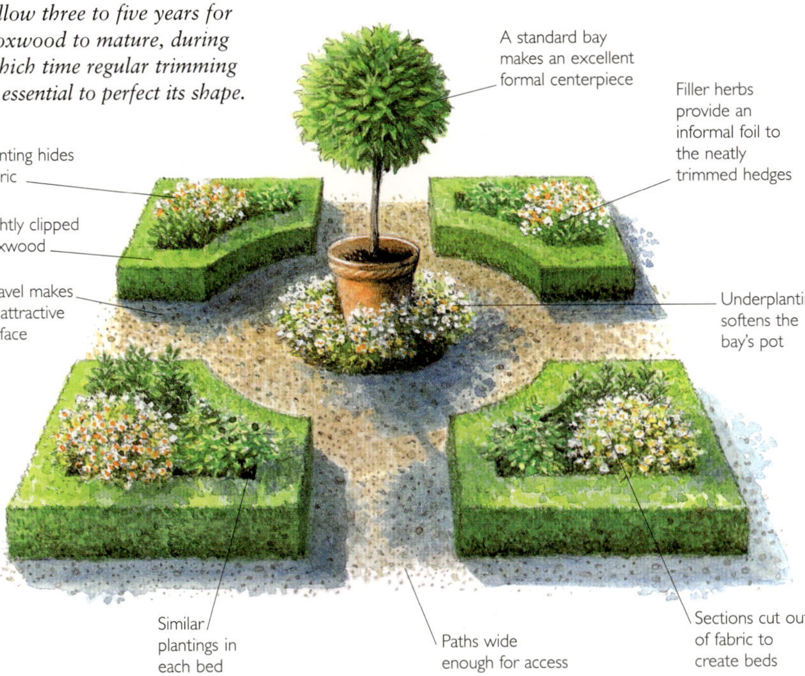

◀ GRAND STYLE *Chives and lavender cotton alternate as filling between boxwood hedges.*

YOU NEED:

TOOLS
- Club hammer
- Tape measure
- Builder's square
- Scissors
- Fork • Spade
- Trowel
- Permanent marker pen
- Wire cutters

MATERIALS
- Marker pegs
- String
- 12×12ft/3.5×3.5m sheet of landscape fabric
- Galvanized wire
- 220lb/100kg gravel

WORKING PLAN

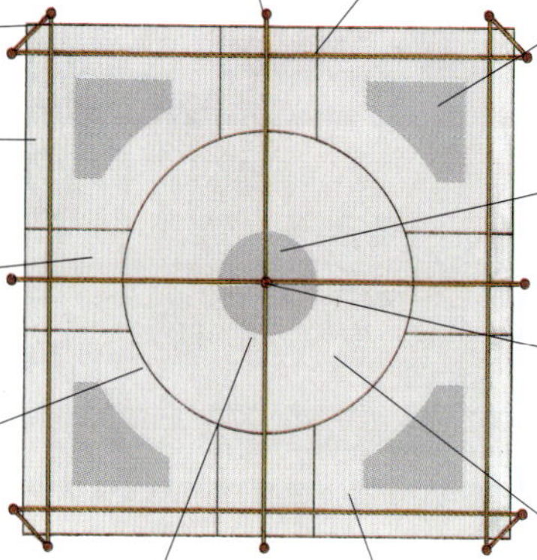

MARKING OUT AND LAYING LANDSCAPE FABRIC

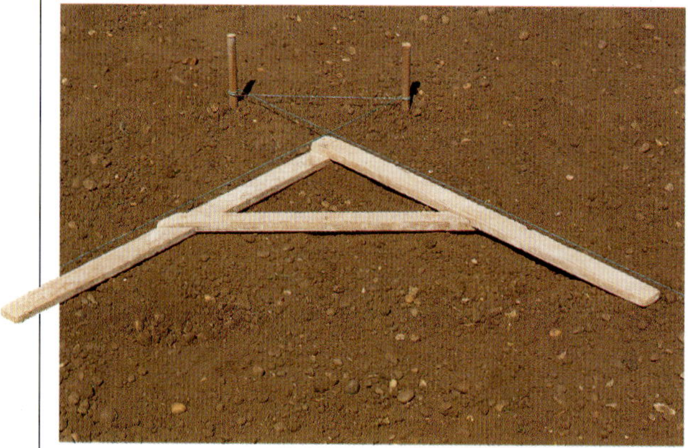

1 Mark out a perfect square for the outer boxwood edging (sheets of fabric make unreliable guides). Lay a builder's square on the ground where you want the "first" corner, and hammer pegs 6in/15cm beyond each edge. Wind string around them to cross as shown at the square's tip. Measure 10½ft/3.2m along the string, place the square and repeat, then take the string on until all four sides are formed.

2 Ease the sheet of fabric under the string square, pulling it flat and trimming if necessary. Leave a generous overlap beyond the guide – the surplus fabric will give the roots of the young boxwood protection on the outer edge of the garden and can be concealed with soil or a sod, gravel, or paved edging.

Finding the Center and Securing Fabric

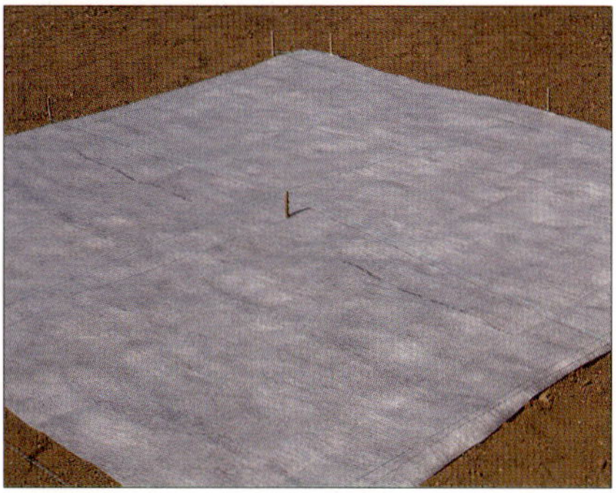

1 To find the center of the site, you need to find the midpoint of each side. With these dimensions, it will be 5¼ft/1.6m from the corner made by the crossing string. Hammer a peg into the ground to mark the position.

2 Run lengths of string between the pairs of opposite pegs so that they form a cross. The point at which the lines meet is the center of the square. Insert a peg at this point, piercing the material first (*see below*).

3 Secure the fabric at approximately 12in/30cm intervals with lengths of wire bent into hoops. Always use the end of the wire or an awl to pierce holes in the fabric before hammering hooks or pegs through it. This puts less strain on the material and prevents it from bunching up.

Marking Out the Paths

1 To mark the central circular path, tie a length of string to the central peg and make knots at 12in/30cm and 36in/90cm from the peg. Hold the marker pen against the knots and inscribe the circles.

2 Mark out the four paths by measuring 12in/30cm either side of the string guides that cross at the center. Use a permanent marker and the builder's square to ensure that the lines are straight and right angles are true.

CUTTING AWAY FABRIC AND PLANTING

1 Cut away the landscape fabric for the four areas to be planted with filler herbs, leaving a 4in/10cm overlap of fabric within the beds. Also, cut from the central disk if desired. Peg the fabric down at intervals with wire hooks, as before.

2 Position the boxwood plants around the path edges and perimeter, spacing them approximately 3in/8cm apart. Mark their positions and cut crosses in the fabric. Open up the crosses, make holes, plant the boxwood, then water well.

PLANTS AND FABRIC

Landscape fabric has a huge advantage over other more economical materials used to suppress weeds, such as black plastic, because it allows water through into the soil, while still minimizing its loss the other way – from the soil into the atmosphere. It is available in rolls of various widths in most garden centers; lengths can be overlapped over large areas.

3 Walk along the path areas to compact the soil, remove the string, and spread a ½in/1cm layer of gravel (or bark chips) on the paths and around the boxwood. As well as hiding the fabric, it will keep the roots of the boxwood plants cool.

4 Arrange the filler herbs in their positions, having first watered each plant thoroughly. Then remove them from their pots and plant. During the dry season, water regularly until the knot garden is established.

HERBS USED

EDGING
100 Boxwood

FILLING
8 Gingermint
12 Golden feverfew
16 Variegated lemon balm

BLOCKS OF COLOR

Most people fill in formally edged beds with a variety of plants, but for real impact, group dense, low plants of the same type closely to form striking patchwork designs. With open-knot designs *(illustrated below)*, the color of the path material can also play a part. A closed-knot design *(see photograph, below right)* has broader, interlaced hedges and beds, with no room for paths; closed knots are very difficult to tend but do look superb.

CREATING SINGLE BLOCKS OF COLOR

SQUARED UP
Purple and green-leaved basil provide the beds' color theme, while blue-flowered hyssop draws the eye to the center of this design.

CROSSING PATHS
Here, the contrast between blocks of purple (lavender) and yellow-gold (santolina in flower) produces a wonderfully vibrant effect.

TEXTURED TRIANGLES
Each section in this design could be filled with a variety of thymes and sages, creating an elegant assortment of green, gold, and purple.

HERBS FOR KNOT GARDENS

FOR EDGING
These plants have an upright habit and can tolerate regular clipping:
Boxwood
Curry plant
Hyssop
Lavender
Rosemary
Santolina
Wall germander

FOR FILLING
The following will add blocks of color:
Golden-leaved herbs
Golden marjoram
Golden feverfew
Silver-leaved herbs
Curry plant
Santolina
Variegated herbs
Variegated meadow-sweet
Variegated lemon balm
Flowering herbs
Hyssop
Sage
Wall germander

CLOSED-KNOT GARDEN
Here, three types of hedging herb – boxwood, sage, and santolina – have been used to create a closed-knot pattern.

HERBS WITH PAVING

PAVING BEDDED ON SAND creates ideal conditions for herbs that like sunny, fast-draining ground. Creeping herbs such as thyme will spread out from the cracks, or you can plant self-seeders such as golden feverfew to germinate in crevices. A custom-built checkerboard pattern of slabs with herbs in the spaces between is both decorative and practical, giving easy access to each plant. Alternatively, you can plant herbs in and around existing paving (*see p.33*).

CHECKERBOARD HERB GARDEN

This simple design makes an extremely effective showpiece for herbs, planted to create blocks of color that highlight the design. Slabs are placed alternately with gaps over an area whose size depends on the measurements and number of the slabs used.

PLANTING TIPS

- Always include herbs with a spreading or naturally floppy habit to soften the hard edges of the paving slabs.
- A checkerboard is a good place to grow spreading herbs, such as mint, which will be contained by the paving slabs.

YOU NEED:

TOOLS

- Pegs, string, builder's square, straightedge
- Spade • Rake
- Club hammer
- Hammer
- Level
- Builder's trowel
- Fork

MATERIALS

- 4 boards of 4×¾in/10×2cm treated lumber, two of them 92in/2.3m long and two 72in/1.8m long
- 8 wooden pegs, 2×2×12in/5×5×30cm
- 12 2¾in/7cm galvanized nails
- 13 50lb/25kg bags of sharp (horticultural) sand
- 10 slabs, each 18×18×1¼in/45×45×3cm
- 50lb/25kg mortar mix

CONSTRUCTION PLAN
The template for this design is simple but effective. With 10 slabs arranged like this, the strips of wood edging the feature need to be four times and just over five times the width of a slab.

◀ SOFT EDGES *Billowing planting and weathered slabs soon make the feature look mature.*

PREPARING THE SITE AND FRAMEWORK

1 Mark the perimeter (92×74in/2.3×1.85m) with string and pegs (*detail on p.24*). Dig out soil to the same depth as the edging boards (4in/10cm); keep it for the planting spaces.

2 Rake the area smooth and as level as possible, removing large stones. Work backward so that you step on the soil as little as possible and do not compact it.

3 Place the boards around the edges of the rectangle, pushing them firmly in position. Hammer a peg inside one of the corners so that its top is 1¼in/3cm lower than the top of the boards. Put in another peg in the same way, approximately half-way along the side.

4 Use a level to check that the tops of the boards are level. (This is very important, since the slabs must lie flush with the wooden edging.) Work your way around the rectangle, putting pegs in each of the corners and down the sides. Nail the boards to the pegs to secure them.

ADDING THE SAND AND ARRANGING THE SLABS

1 Cover the base of the area with a 2in/5cm layer of sharp sand. This helps make a level, firm foundation for laying the paving slabs.

2 Smooth out and press down the sand using the straightedge. Pull the straightedge firmly toward you to get a level surface, and check it with a level. Work backward to avoid stepping on the sand.

3 Lay all of the slabs in position, leaving an 18in/45cm gap (the length of a slab) between each one. At this stage the slabs will be slightly lower than the edging to allow space for a layer of mortar. Mix the sand-cement mixture with sufficient water to make a fairly stiff mortar.

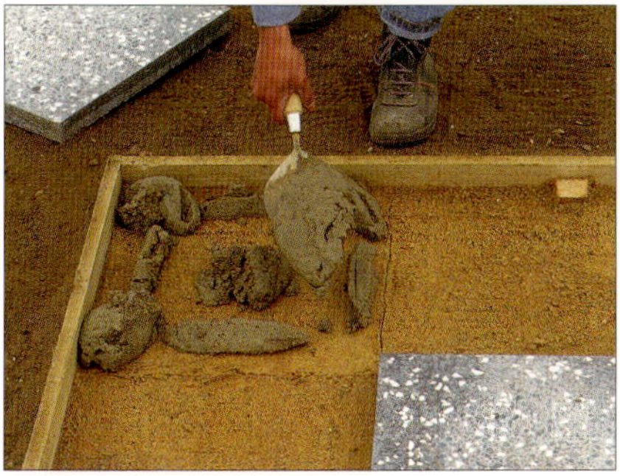

4 Lift the slabs one at a time and place blobs of mortar in each corner, in the middle, and along the inside edge of each space. This will secure the slabs.

5 Position each slab, tamping it down with the handle of the club hammer against a piece of wood. Check with a level, making sure the slab aligns with the frame.

PREPARING FOR PLANTING

1 When all the slabs are laid, scoop sand away from around their edges and seal with mortar to keep them securely in place. Allow a little time for the mortar to set.

2 Fill the planting areas with the retained soil, forking it over so that it is evenly mixed with the sand. Make sure the mortar is fully set before stepping on the slabs to plant.

MATERIALS AND PLANTS

Paving slabs come in a wide range of colors, sizes, shapes, and textures. They can be made from natural stone or cement and can be smooth or textured. You can combine several different paving materials and shapes to create an informal effect, or you may prefer to keep the design uniform. Whatever you decide, it is always best to use materials that blend well with surrounding buildings and with the herbs you plan to plant.

TYPES OF PAVING SLAB
Slabs are usually square or rectangular, but other shapes are available. Natural stone blends into a garden better than artificial materials, but it is expensive. Textured cement, however, gives a reasonably natural effect at much lower cost.

FILLER HERBS

Basil (*Ocimum*)
Bee balm (*Monarda*)
Borage (*Borago*)
Chamomile (*Chamaemelum*)
Chives (*Allium schoenoprasum*)
Dill (*Anethum*)
Wall germander (*Teucrium*)
Hyssop (*Hyssopus*)
Lavender (*Lavandula*)
Lemon balm (*Melissa*)
Marjoram (*Origanum*)
Mint (*Mentha*)
Nasturtiums (*Tropaeolum*)
Pot marigolds (*Calendula*)
Sage (*Salvia*)
Lavender cotton (*Santolina*)
Tansy (*Tanacetum*)

ADAPTING EXISTING PAVING

Existing slabs can often be lifted to make planting spaces for herbs, especially if the paving is not securely laid. The soil underneath needs to be forked over and improved before planting. Or, if cracks are large enough, you can plant low-growing herbs that tolerate being occasionally stepped on.

LIFTING SLABS FROM PAVED AREAS

1 **Scrape out** and clear away any debris or old mortar around the slab. Insert a spade into the gap along one edge, then lever up the slab and remove it.

2 **Remove any gravel** and compacted soil under the slab. Loosen and aerate the remaining soil with a fork if it is of reasonable quality; otherwise, remove it.

3 **Fill the planting area** with a mixture of topsoil, compost, and sharp sand. Level the surface so that it is ready for sowing seeds or planting your herbs.

PLANTING BETWEEN PAVING SLABS

HERBS IN CREVICES

Creeping thymes are ideal in paving. Plants can be inserted if gaps are wide enough, or you can sow seed (see inset). *Clear out the crevice, fill with soil, water, scatter seeds, and water again.*

CREVICE HERBS

- Compact marjoram, such as *Origanum vulgare* 'Compactum'
- Creeping mint
- Creeping savory
- Creeping thyme
- Dwarf feverfew, such as *Tanacetum parthenium* 'Golden Moss'
- Chamomile

HERBS IN BRICK PATTERNS

BEDS EDGED WITH CLIPPED BOXWOOD look splendid but take years to perfect. For a formal herb feature that will take only a day to build and a season to mature, use bricks to edge beds. In a wide range of textures and colors, you can use them to create all kinds of shapes and patterns, and you can mix in other materials (*see pp.38–39*). The brick lines could be used to separate blocks of different foliage colors or types of herb, or mix plants for a less formal effect.

MAKING AN HERB WHEEL

This traditional, visually effective design can be built in less than a day, and the materials used are not expensive. The mortar mix is used dry, so it is much easier and less messy to work with. The only preparation needed is to level and rake the site. The wheel featured here is 5ft/1.5m across, allowing plenty of room for herbs. A large plant or an ornament – perhaps a birdbath or a sundial (*see p.9*) – makes a central focal point.

YOU NEED:

TOOLS
- Rake
- Spade
- Club hammer
- Straightedge
- Level
- Trowel
- Marking pegs
- String
- Tape measure

MATERIALS
- Sharp sand
- 50 landscape bricks (8½x4x2½in/ 22x10x6cm)
- 275lb/125kg mortar mix (1 part cement to 6 parts builder's sand)

PLANTING A WHEEL
Low, symmetrical planting with height in the center would suit an island bed, but if your wheel is by a wall or in a corner, you can position taller plants toward the back.

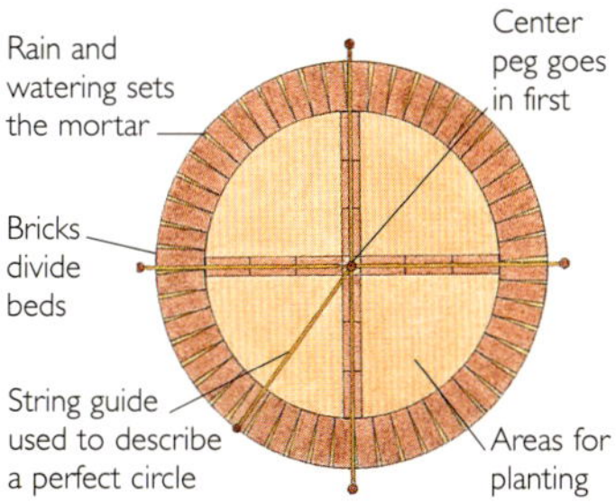

WORKING PLAN

MATCHING MATERIALS *You can choose bricks to blend in with existing paths and walls.*

Marking and Digging Out the Circle

1 To mark out the edge, place a peg roughly in the center of the site. Tie a length of string to the peg and then tie a knot at half the width you want the herb bed area to be (here 27½in/70cm). Hold a peg against the knot and inscribe a circle around the center peg; trickle sand over it (*inset*) to mark it clearly.

2 Starting on the circle mark and working outward, dig out a shallow trench, just wider and 2in/5cm deeper than your bricks. This will allow plenty of space for both the bricks and the layer of dry mortar mix ("lean" mix) below that secures them. Keep some of the dug-out soil for filling in later.

Positioning and Laying Bricks

1 Arrange all the bricks around the trench first so that you can adjust spacing where needed. The bigger the circle, the smaller the gaps between bricks at the outer edges will be.

2 Spread a 2in/5cm layer of the mortar mix over the base of the trench and, placing three or four bricks at a time, tap into position. Use a level to check their placement.

3 **To position the spokes,** divide the wheel in half by putting in 2 pegs outside it and joining them with string, which must also pass the center peg. Repeat to make quarters and check with a builder's square.

4 **Dig trenches** for the spokes, just wider and deeper than the bricks. Set the bricks on a layer of mortar mix, then pack soil up against them. You can either complete the cross or leave a central hole for a plant.

Spacing and Planting the Herbs

Arrange the plants in their positions before you plant, then adjust spacing as required. Water thoroughly, then remove each plant from its pot by tapping the base and pulling gently. Make planting holes and insert the plants, then water them in well. Water regularly until the young plants are fully established, especially in dry weather.

HERBS USED IN THE BEDS

3 Bronze fennel	3 Borage
3 Chives	4 Marjoram
2 Spearmint	5 Chamomile
5 Thyme	3 Golden feverfew

Alternative Brick Patterns

Bricks laid flat in lines, end to end, can be used to mark out all sorts of designs (*see below*) at the least expense, but you can also vary the way they are laid to add interest to edging. Double rows can be laid end on, then side on for a basketweave pattern, or diagonally, herringbone-style. Try alternating bricks laid flat with bricks on their ends sticking up between them for mini-battlements, or sink them part-way into the soil at an angle for a sawtooth effect. Bricks also mix well with a variety of other materials.

Style Decisions

Always choose bricks that relate in color and texture to the existing hard surfaces of your house and garden for a unified effect. A builder's supply store may well have a wider selection than most home and garden centers. The texture of the bricks is also important; smooth, new bricks could look great in a modern garden design, but rough-textured facing bricks, which already appear weathered, are more appropriate in a traditional or cottage-style setting. They also give a firmer footing; for a nonslip surface, use stable bricks, attractively etched with crisscrossing diagonal lines.

BUYING BRICKS

The types of brick that flake through frost damage are unsuitable for paving, but if used ornamentally they will age and "distress" quickly, if that is the look you desire.

- "Engineering" bricks, flat on both sides, are hard-wearing and frost- and moisture-resistant.
- "Frogged" bricks, usually also weatherproof, are the ones with a dent (the "frog").
- "Facing" bricks, usually shallower, are used for decorative coverings; not all can withstand severe weather. The bricks with three holes along their length are known as "cored" – with already-made planting pockets!

DOUBLE DIAMOND
This bold design could be set into a patio as a planting feature. You will need a builder's square to ensure true right angles.

SQUARED CIRCLE
Make a circle as for a wheel, and use string guides to divide it into six beds. Cut off the outer curved segments with bricks for a hexagonal shape.

BRICK LADDER
Planted with tough, creeping herbs such as thymes, this ladder could be set into an infrequently used path. Make sure soil and bricks are level.

Combining Materials

Small herb-bed features provide an opportunity to introduce interesting hard landscaping materials into the garden without laying out too much money, particularly when set off by less expensive materials such as gravel or cobblestones set in mortar. When combining more than two materials, as below, try to match at least two in color or texture, or the result will be too busy, especially in small spaces. Modern, "antiqued" pavers and rope- or barley-twist edging are very convincing, or you might want to invest a little more in originals. Salvage yards often have small quantities of reclaimed pavers or edging tiles that, because they do not interest professionals working on large projects, may be quite modestly priced.

▶ FILLING GAPS
Dyes are available to make mortars blend in, here between square pavers – or you could choose a contrasting color for a more lively effect. Make wide gaps more interesting by studding the mortar with small pebbles, seashells, or even terracotta pot shards.

LOOSE SURFACES
Use frogged bricks either face down or on their sides, especially next to soil or other materials that tend to "travel," such as gravel.

Mediterranean Style

The sun-loving herbs that thrive on Mediterranean hillsides are ideally suited to hot, stony ground. A stony layer over the soil is not only a natural way to conserve moisture, but it also absorbs the sun's warmth during the day to release it at night, creating a favorable microclimate. Build a scree garden (*below*) or grow spreading herbs, such as thyme, near paths or other hard surfaces so they can inch their way into crannies or along the cracks in a flight of steps.

Making a Scree Garden

A scree garden mimics the rocky natural landscape at the foot of a hill or cliff. It is an ideal feature for areas of low rainfall, but, to make it look natural and maximize its water-saving properties, it is important to position rocks and plants as shown below. When angled correctly, the rocks channel rainwater toward the plants instead of letting it roll down the slope.

Choose rocks of a type and color to blend into your surroundings. Good suppliers should be able to guarantee that they do not come from an area where their extraction may damage the environment – more important in some areas than in others. The mock tufa and reconstituted rocks now available are both cheap and convincing.

PRACTICAL TIPS

- Do not use rocks too heavy for you to handle comfortably, and do not bend from the waist or use a twisting movement if lifting, since you can damage your back.
- For the best effect, choose a site where a wall or fence can act as backdrop.
- Select the sunniest spot possible, since heat will intensify the plants' aromas.

HOW A SCREE GARDEN WORKS
It is essential that the rocks are positioned in a natural-looking way but also at an angle that gives maximum benefit to the plants.

SCREE GARDEN *Rocks and stones provide a natural setting for sun-loving herbs.*

YOU NEED:

TOOLS

- Spade
- Rake
- Trowel

MATERIALS

- Sharp sand
- Rocks of varying sizes, generally about 6×12in/15×30cm here, where sandstone is used
- Scree – a range of small stones, from about ¾–2½in/2–6cm. 50lb/25kg should cover about 10sq ft/1sq m.

ARRANGING THE ROCKS

1 **Having weeded** and dug the site, spread a 1in/2.5cm layer of sharp sand over the surface. Dig it into the soil to assist drainage.

2 **Rake soil** toward the back of the area, to create a gentle slope. Choose a gradient that is appropriate to the site.

3 **Position the large rocks,** arranging them in as naturalistic a way as possible. Some may need to be grouped together, with others set a little way apart.

4 **Dig a shallow depression** for each rock. Make sure that when in position the rock is at the correct angle to the slope (*see previous page*) and sits securely in the ground.

5 **Place the herbs,** still in their pots, in their planting positions. Make sure that the larger plants are each put behind a rock so that their roots keep cool and can absorb all the available moisture. Place small plants toward the front of the site.

Planting Herbs and Spreading Scree

1 **Dig planting holes** for the larger herbs. Ease them from their pots, then plant to the correct depth. Firm the soil around each plant and water in thoroughly.

2 **Pile the larger pieces** of scree among the rocks in this part of the bed. Then, using a rake, distribute the pieces evenly over the area, taking care not to damage the plants.

3 **Use a trowel** to make planting holes for the smaller herbs. Remove from their pots, plant, and water.

4 **Cover the lower,** front part of the bed with the smallest grade of scree. Use a trowel to spread the stones carefully among and around the plants without damaging them.

AROMATIC ENVIRONMENT

In the finished garden, silver-leaved herbs blend with the pale-colored scree. The sun will draw out the herbs' full aroma. Little maintenance will be needed: remove any weeds that do appear as soon as seen.

HERBS USED

Artemisia

Lavender (several types, including English lavender, *Lavandula angustifolia*)

Lavender cotton

Rosemary

Sage (including pineapple sage, *S. elegans*, and golden-variegated sage, *Salvia officinalis* 'Icterina')

Thyme

PLANTING POSSIBILITIES

Herb plants and stones make perfect companions, and not just in rock gardens and scree gardens. Paths, walls, and steps all provide opportunities to use herbs that will bask in reflected warmth, while their roots creep under stones and into crevices to seek moist soil and protection from the heat of the sun. Also, such situations usually offer good drainage and thus protection from winter moisture, which many sun-loving herbs dislike.

PLANTING HERBS AMONG STEPS

You may have steps where a path changes in level, or you could incorporate a couple into a rock or scree garden design for interest and access. Around them, grow spreading, creeping herbs such as thymes, catmints, and chamomile to soften the edges and colonize cracks (some will self-seed, too), but trim them back from time to time so that the steps do not become dangerous, especially in wet weather.

A FIRM FOOTING
If you are planning to use rough-hewn rocks to form steps along a path, make the treads really wide and easy to negotiate.

SAFE SURFACES
Even if steps don't go anywhere in particular, keep rocky surfaces moss- and algae-free, and don't let plants cover them completely.

BUILDING SIMPLE STEPS

Incorporating some informal steps into a sloping rock or scree garden gives you easy access to tend plants. Choose flattish stones that are of the same type and color as the other rocks to retain the steps, cementing them in on a simple footing of crushed stone. Pack soil behind them and make flat treads with a layer of mortar studded with rounded pebbles, again in a matching stone. Planting pockets will really help blend the steps into the feature.

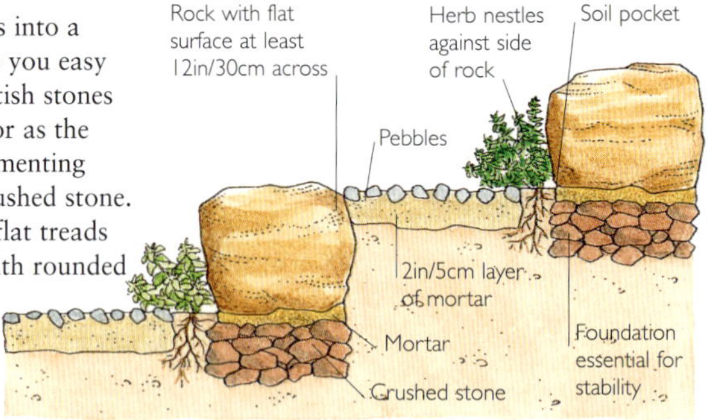

Associating Plants with Stone

The most successful gardens not only group different plants together well but also associate hard landscaping materials with plants to create contrasts of color and texture. Rocks, stones, pebbles, or gravel that you introduce into your garden should match what exists locally, both in terms of the soil and of building materials; you will find, with experimentation, that certain plants not only complement but are flattered by them. A little research into the native habitat of plants can contribute to ideas for creating a landscape in which the planting looks very natural.

◀ WINDSWEPT MOOR
Tufa is a neutral, natural foil for tough, wiry, acid-hating thymes. For a really long-established effect, you can hollow out planting pockets in this soft stone.

TUFA

▶ BRIGHT AND BREEZY
To accentuate a coastal feel in a planting on sandy soil, use low, sun-loving, wind-resistant plants in bold colors. Golden foliage always adds warmth and light.

SANDSTONE

◀ DARK AND HANDSOME
Slate landscapes are often associated with running water and lush growth: use vivid, vigorous foliage herbs such as bronze fennel, mint, and artemisia, here with sedums.

SLATE

Herbs in Containers

WINDOWBOXES, POTS, AND PLANTERS are ideal for growing herbs if space is limited. Position them wherever they are useful or look decorative – on steps, sills, or secured to balcony railings. You can keep culinary herbs close to the kitchen, or use aromatic plants to scent a patio. Clipped into globes and cones (*see p.50*), boxwood and bay make perfect centerpieces for formal gardens. Site tender and sun-loving herbs, such as basil and thymes, in the sunniest spots.

Windowbox Herb Garden

This miniature herb bed (*left*) can be packed with plants to use all summer. They will need more care than if growing in the ground. Plant soft-stemmed herbs that you will harvest often, such as parsley and chives, or choose small plants of larger, shrubby herbs such as rosemary, marjoram, and thyme and, at the end of the season, plant them out or bring them indoors.

Planting a Windowbox

YOU NEED:

TOOLS
- Trowel
- Bucket

MATERIALS
- Windowbox
- Drainage pieces
- Sharp sand
- Multipurpose soil mix

1 **Cover the base** of the trough with a layer of broken terracotta crocks to ensure good drainage, which is essential for most herbs. (Pieces of screening, a layer of chunky gravel, or pebbles make good alternatives.)

2 **Using a trowel,** mix together five parts by volume potting mix to one part sharp sand.

3 **Fill the windowbox** with the soil mix and sand mixture until it is about two-thirds full. This should leave sufficient depth to set in small herb plants and to pack adequate soil mix around their rootballs.

◄ CORE COLLECTION *A single container can provide a wide range of culinary flavors.*

Positioning the Plants

1 Before planting, arrange the herbs in their pots alongside the windowbox in their approximate positions. Bear in mind heights and growth habits; for example, put trailing plants at the front. Water the plants well before removing them from their pots.

PLANTS USED

- 1 Chives
- 1 French tarragon
- 1 Garlic chives
- 1 Oregano
- 1 Rosemary
- 1 Sage
- 1 Spearmint
- 2 Thyme

2 Remove each plant from its pot only when you are ready to plant it, squeezing the sides of the pot and gently pulling it out. If you encounter any resistance, tap the pot firmly, then try again until the plant slides out easily.

3 Make planting holes with your hand, and insert the plants. Add more soil mix to within 1½–2in/4–5cm of the rim (to leave room for watering). Firm around the plants to ensure there are no air pockets, add more mix if necessary, then water well. As the herbs grow, water and trim or harvest them regularly. At the end of the season, plant out the hardy herbs.

AN HERB CASCADE

This unusual way of using simple clay pots can create a charming effect as the plants mature. Trailing herbs planted in the lowest tier will tumble over the sides, while silver-leaved thymes and fresh green marjorams can provide ruffs of foliage interest. Alpine strawberries, as used here, make a mouthwatering addition.

PREPARING THE BASE

YOU NEED:

TOOLS
- Trowel

MATERIALS
- 5 terracotta pots with the following diameters: 15in/39cm, 12in/32cm, 10in/27cm, 8in/21cm, and 6in/16cm
- Broken clay pots
- Soil mix: 5 parts multipurpose mix by volume to 1 part sharp sand

1 **Cover the base** of the largest pot with a layer of broken pots to assist drainage. If plants are in constantly soggy soil mix, the roots may eventually rot.

2 **Add a generous layer** of the thoroughly mixed soil mix and sand, so that the broken pot pieces are completely covered. Roughly level out the surface.

ARRANGING THE POTS

1 **Sit the next largest pot** inside, touching one side, so that the base of its rim aligns with the top of the first pot. Adjust the soil mix level to achieve the right height.

2 **Keeping the second pot** firm and level, fill the base pot up with the soil mix. Firm as you fill, tapping the pot to encourage the mix to settle evenly.

3 **Repeat the process** using the other pots until the cascade is complete. Arrange the pots asymmetrically as before to leave wider planting spaces for the herbs.

Planting the Tiers

Plant up each tier, starting at the bottom and spacing the herbs so that they can spread a little. Water thoroughly.

PLANTS USED

5 Alpine strawberries
2 Basil
2 Pot marjoram
1 Oregano
3 Gold-leaved thyme
3 Silver-leaved thyme

More Container Ideas

You can use all sorts of containers for herbs, provided that they have holes for drainage in the bottom. A clipped evergreen in a good-sized pot, in balance with the size of its head of growth, will last for years if fed every spring and well watered. Closely planted herbs will need lifting and possibly renewing every year.

Clipped Bay Trees

You only need clip bay twice, in late spring and late summer. Bay leaves retain their flavor exceptionally well: stored in an airtight container, the clippings should last all year round. A top-dressing of fresh soil mix and the addition of some slow-release fertilizer granules each spring will keep growth vigorous.

▶ STANDARD BAY
Bays can be bought as standards to make long-lasting feature plants. Variegated thymes make a nice underplanting.

OTHER HERBS FOR SHAPING

Bay makes the most effective standard plants, but other shrubby herbs can be grown clipped into neat bun shapes for formal display. Choose any of the plants recommended for formal edging (*see p.27*).

Using a Strawberry Jar

These attractive planters are equally suited to growing herbs, and they also use space to best advantage. Choose small-size pots of herbs so that, holding the topgrowth gently bunched in one hand, you can insert the rootballs through the planting holes in the side. Do not fill the pot completely with soil mix then try to force the plants in through the side: add a layer of mix up to the level of the first hole, then plant, then add another layer, and so on (*see below left*). Then plant the top layer.

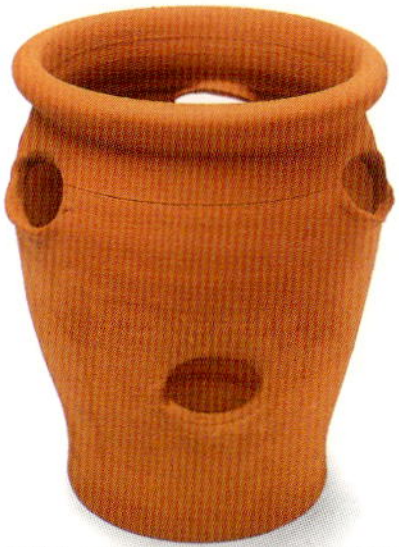

◄PLANT CARE
Keep terracotta pots well watered from the top, since the soil mix around the planting holes can easily dry out through the porous terracotta.

▼PLANTING UP IN STAGES
With one hand in and one hand out of the planter, ease in the plants and firm soil mix up, under, and around their rootballs.

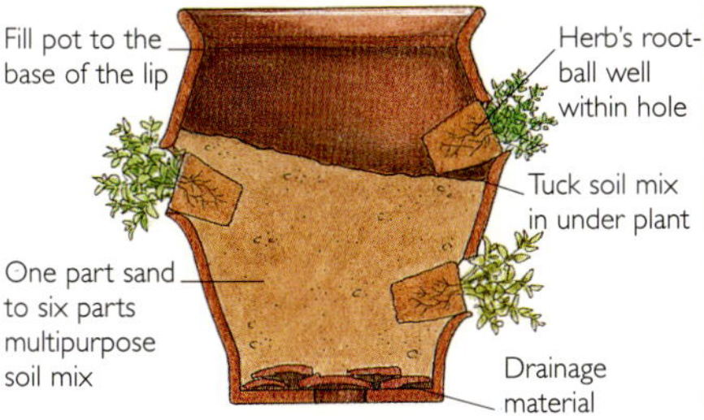

GOOD MIXERS
Alpine strawberries, which are not too vigorous, make perfect partners in this pot for tarragon, rosemary, savory, and marjoram.

An Herb Tower

This tall wire basket has been converted into a planter by lining it with a thick layer of sphagnum moss (felt or fiber hanging-basket liner makes a good substitute), then plastic pierced with plenty of holes at the base. Add drainage material at the base, then fill with a free-draining soil mix, as for other containers. You can use wire-cutters to snip out planting holes in the side (not too many, or you will weaken the structure), being sure to clip off or bend over any spikes of wire for safety. Plant creeping herbs such as thyme around the sides to trail down and give the tower a truly natural look. Keep it well watered.

LOOKING AFTER HERB PLANTS

PREPARING AND PLANTING

HERBS DO NOT DEMAND LOTS OF NOURISHMENT; provided the soil has been dug over and weeded, most will grow happily without additional fertilizers. Choose plants to match your soil (*below*), and water them well upon planting and during their first spring and summer, particularly in hot spells. Given a good start, these easygoing plants are easy to tend and trouble-free.

WHICH HERBS FOR YOUR SOIL?

To save yourself the most work, choose herbs that will enjoy your garden soil. Feverfew, parsley, chives, and mint like rich, cool soil, but in heavy ground in a cold, wet winter, the roots of sun-loving herbs such as rosemary, sage, and lavender may rot away. You can improve a heavy soil at planting (*below*), but light soil will need continual bulking up with organic matter.

GROWING TIP

If your soil is unsuitable for certain herbs, consider growing them in containers. Tough, sun-loving herbs will be happy in a light, gritty soil mix and will tolerate a certain amount of summer neglect. Leafy herbs such as parsley need spongy, moisture-retentive soil mix and plenty of water.

IMPROVING DRAINAGE

Mediterranean herbs like to snake their roots through free-draining, stony ground. To lighten up a clay soil, add plenty of sand or grit, preferably over the whole planting area before you plant it up, or by working it into the base and sides of planting holes. You must use sharp sand (not soft builder's sand, which clumps together and spoils the soil's texture); this may be called "garden" or "horticultural" sand at home and garden centers. Similarly, choose "garden" grit if available, that has been washed free of lime, which many of these plants dislike. Remember that more freely draining soil requires more watering.

SHARP SAND

COARSE GRIT

ADDING SAND OR GRIT
Mix in the drainage material well before you plant. The heavier the soil, the more sand or grit will be required.

Spacing and Planting Out Young Plants

Close planting means that beds will fill out quickly, but it tends to lead to more work as plants begin to crowd each other. Wide spacing will leave gaps in which weeds are likely to grow. Check plant labels to see what the eventual spread and height of each plant will be, and space appropriately.

SPACING TIPS

- To relieve crowding, you need to lift plants and divide or even replace them. Pruning will only make them grow even more vigorously.
- Check labels to look for smaller or more slow-growing varieties of the herbs you want.

ARRANGING AND PLANTING *Arrange the herbs in their pots first, giving each enough room to grow and considering how much you want them to spill over the edges of the planting area. Water the herbs, plant and firm in, then water again.*

Controlling Invasive Herbs

Some herbs, especially mints, can spread at a rapid rate, swamping other plants. The best way to restrict them is to plant them in a sunken pot, providing a physical barrier so that spreading runners cannot escape. Divide the plants each spring and refill the pot with fresh soil or soil mix or a combination of the two, then replant.

1 **Dig a hole** large enough to hold a big container with drainage holes. Place it in the hole and add soil mix.

2 **Plant the herb** (*here mint*) in the pot and firm. Add enough soil mix to cover the pot's rim, and water well.

INVASIVE HERBS

Herbs that, in small spaces, need to be kept in check and regularly divided (*see p.57*) include:

Comfrey
Marjoram
Mint
Tarragon (especially Russian)
Tansy
Thyme
Sweet woodruff

Caring for Herbs

Healthy young plants are quick to thrive and, if they have been planted carefully in well-prepared soil, will require little aftercare. Water well for the first few weeks; if the soil is merely dampened, roots stay near the surface instead of penetrating deep into the ground. Once established, harvest leaves and shoots regularly to encourage bushy, fresh growth.

Encouraging Healthy Plants

Few popular herbs are big feeders, but if harvested heavily and often they will need fertilizer. Pinching out shoot tips will encourage leafy herbs to produce plenty of fresh foliage, while shrubby herbs need trimming once or twice a year to keep them in good shape. With some herbs it is better to remove flowers in bud to preserve a good flavor; others need deadheading.

TIPS FOR GOOD GROWTH

- Do not harvest newly planted herbs until they are established and making new growth.
- Grow sufficient quantities of culinary favorites (*see pp.12–15*) so that plants do not suffer from being cut too hard, too often.
- During hot or windy weather, make sure that herbs in pots receive sufficient water.

TRIMMING
Trim gray-leaved herbs such as lavender twice a year. In autumn, remove dead flowers and cut back leggy stems (right)*. The following spring, clip at least 1in/2.5cm of the previous year's growth* (far right)*, making sure some foliage remains.*

KEEPING HERBS IN GOOD SHAPE

NIPPING BUDS

Remove flower buds to prevent bitterness in cooking:
Arugula, basil, lovage, parsley, salad burnet, tarragon.
Remove flower buds from **chives** to encourage new foliage (although if you let them flower you can use the flowerheads in salads and omelettes).

DEADHEADING

Deadhead to prevent self-seeding:
Angelica, borage, dill, evening primroses, fennel, feverfew, garlic chives, lemon balm.
Deadhead to prolong flowering season:
Borage, catmint, nasturtiums, pot marigolds.

PINCHING OUT

Pinch out or harvest regularly to promote bushy new foliage:
Basil, lemon balm, lovage, marjoram, mint, parsley, sage, salad burnet, sweet cicely, thyme.
Leggy lemon balms, chives, and mints can be cut back with shears to encourage fresh new growth.

PRUNING

Trim twice a year (*see above*) to keep plants in good shape:
Curry plant, lavender, winter savory, santolina.
Cut back almost to ground level once or twice in the growing season to prolong the life of the plants:
Angelica, fennel, marjoram, mint.

Growing Herbs for Winter Use

While most herbs are harvested from spring to autumn, dying down over winter outside, some can be lifted (*below*) and grown inside on a windowsill or in a greenhouse. Pots of late summer-sown herbs (*see next page*) such as cilantro and parsley will grow well on a warm, sunny sill. Where hardy (or if grown indoors), evergreen herbs can be harvested throughout winter. Although there will be no fresh growth, the leaves are still flavorsome.

SUPERMARKET POTS

The small pots of growing herbs available from supermarkets can be used to supplement winter supplies and also provide a source of new plants. The pots usually contain a cluster of small plantlets, which are too crowded to survive long. Carefully ease these out of the pot and split them into small plugs, keeping plenty of soil mix attached to their roots. Pot up, water thoroughly, and grow on a bright windowsill.

1 **Herbs that die down** in winter can be lifted for winter use. Choose a dry day in early autumn and, using a fork, lift a mature clump of herbs (*here chives*) from the garden.

2 **Divide the clump** into smaller pieces with your hands. If the plant is tough, use a small, sharp garden knife. Shake firmly to remove loose soil from around the roots.

3 **Plant up** the divided pieces into pots or deep trays of potting mix. Stand them in a saucer, water thoroughly, then discard any excess.

4 **Cut back** any top-growth. Once the leaves have grown to about 4in/10cm, start to harvest them regularly in order to encourage plenty of fresh growth.

HERBS IN WINTER

Evergreens that can be harvested through winter, where hardy (or grown indoors):

Bay, rosemary, sage, thyme, winter savory.

Herbs that can be lifted and brought inside:

Chives, scented geraniums, marjoram, mint, parsley, tarragon.

Herbs to sow and grow on a windowsill:

Arugula, basil, chervil, cilantro, lemon balm, nasturtiums, parsley.

Propagating Your Own Plants

THE MAJORITY OF HERBS can be grown from seed – this method is inexpensive and produces lots of plants. Taking cuttings ensures new plants that are identical to their parents. Division is easy and is a useful way of checking the spread of some herbs. To ensure that newly raised plants are large enough to survive planting out, wait for the root tips to show at the base of the pot.

Sowing Seed

Seed can be sown in containers to produce herbs for planting out, or directly into the open ground; check the back of packets for advice. It can also be sown in the cracks between paving stones (*see p.33*). Spring is the best time for sowing seed, although, if hardy, annuals such as borage may be sown outside in the autumn.

1 **Lightly firm** some multipurpose soil mix, then scatter the seeds. Cover with a light sprinkling of sieved mix. Use a watering can with a fine rose to water in well.

2 **Keep the tray** out of direct sunlight, on a windowsill or in a cold frame, watering or misting regularly. Keep the tray in a pierced plastic bag to keep the humidity level high. When the seedlings start to appear, thin them to about 2in/5cm apart.

3 **When their first leaves** are fully unfurled, carefully lift the seedlings and replant them into small pots of fresh soil mix, carefully holding them by their leaves. Put them back in the frame or on the sill and grow on until large enough to plant out.

Taking Softwood Cuttings

Many shrubby herbs are easily grown from cuttings taken in late spring or early summer. After 6–8 weeks, remove a plant weekly to see if roots are growing; if so, move each into its own pot and grow on until large enough to plant out.

1 **Select a** nonflowering shoot (*here lemon balm*) and cut cleanly just below a leaf joint, 6 leaves down. Trim off the lower leaves.

2 **Make holes,** then insert the cuttings into firmed rooting medium (half peat or peat substitute, half sharp sand). Firm in and water.

3 **Make a tent** with stakes and a pierced plastic bag to keep an even temperature and conserve moisture. Place in a frame or on a shaded sill.

DIVIDING AND MULTIPLYING

For many herbs, dividing is a useful way of creating new plants from older ones that have lost their vigor and become woody and unproductive. Herbs are best divided in early spring or autumn, when not in full growth. Cold periods should be avoided, since it is difficult to reestablish the divided pieces successfully in cold soil.

1 **Insert a fork** well under the plant and lift it clear from the ground. Take care not to damage the roots.

2 **Trim back** heavy top-growth on the sections that you wish to keep, but always leave some foliage.

3 **Divide the clump** into pieces, keeping only the younger, healthier sections, complete with their roots.

4 **Plant the pieces,** spacing them to allow for future spread. Water in and keep the soil moist until established.

ENCOURAGING NEW PLANTLETS

The stems of shrubby herbs, such as thyme and sage, can be encouraged to develop roots by mounding soil mixed with sharp sand and potting mix around the base of the plant in spring, leaving only the shoot tips showing. In late summer or autumn, rooted stems around the plant's edge can be cut off and potted up or planted.

PROPAGATION METHODS FOR POPULAR HERBS

GROWING FROM SEED		CUTTINGS	DIVISION
Angelica	Lovage	Bay	Bee balm
Arugula	Marjoram	French tarragon	Chives
Basil	Pot marigold	Hyssop	Fennel
Borage	Nasturtium	Lavender	French tarragon
Chervil	Parsley	Lemon verbena	Lemon balm
Chives	Sage	Marjoram	Lovage
Cilantro	Savory	Mint	Marjoram
Dill	Sorrel	Rosemary	Mint
Fennel	Sweet cicely	Sage	Thyme
Hyssop	Thyme	Thyme	
Lemon balm		Winter savory	

Drying and Storing Herbs

Many herbs can be dried to make anything from a potpourri to a *bouquet garni* that will add piquancy to a winter casserole. Herbs can also be preserved fresh to recall the scents and flavors of summer. Choose only healthy, pest- and disease-free sprigs while plants are in growth; in autumn, harvest herbaceous herbs to store before they die back or are cut down by frost.

Herbs for Drying

Herbs from hot climates, such as sage, rosemary, and thyme, dry especially well. Soft-leaved herbs, such as basil, take far longer to dry, and some of the flavor may be lost.

Herbs can be air-dried (*below*) in a warm, well-ventilated room. Hang them up or lay out on a rack. They can also be dried in a microwave on a high setting for about four minutes. Alternatively, dry gently in an oven at the very lowest setting. For best flavor, fennel, lovage, mint, rosemary, sage, tarragon, and thyme are best picked before flowering. Hyssop and marjoram should be picked while in flower, while others such as fennel and caraway can be left to produce their spicy, flavorsome seeds.

HARVEST FROM THE GARDEN
Pick herbs for storing early in the day, after any dew or rain has dried. Avoid crushing the leaves in order to preserve their volatile oils.

1 **Most herbs** (here lemon balm) are most easily dried on the stem. Tie into small bunches and hang them upside down in a well-ventilated room.

2 **When the leaves** are brittle and break easily, rub them off the stems onto a sheet of dry paper. Crumble pieces together if you are using the entire plant.

3 **Transfer the dried herbs** to an airtight container, such as a screw-top jar. Use a jar made of colored glass – this helps prevent oxidization, which mars the flavor.

POPULAR HERBS FOR DRYING

Angelica Stems, leaves, and seeds
Bay Leaves
Bee balm Leaves and flowers
Borage Leaves
Catnip, catmint Leaves and flowers
Chamomile Flowers
Chervil Leaves
Chives Leaves and flowers
Coriander Seeds
Curry plant Leaves and flowers
Dill Leaves and seeds
Fennel Leaves and seeds
Geraniums, scented Leaves
Lavender Flowers
Lemon balm Leaves
Lemon verbena Leaves
Lovage Leaves and seeds
Marjoram Leaves and flowers
Mint Leaves
Pot marigold Flowers
Rosemary Leaves
Sage Leaves and flowers
Savory Leaves
Tarragon Leaves
Thyme Leaves and flowers
Yarrow Leaves and flowers

OTHER WAYS OF PRESERVING HERBS

Soft-leaved herbs such as basil, chives, chervil, fennel, and dill retain a better flavor if frozen. Seal them in small plastic bags or, alternatively, lay them in an ice-cube tray, chopping them first if necessary. Fill with water and freeze. Highly aromatic herbs can be preserved in oil, vinegar, syrup, or brandy, imparting their flavor to the liquid at the same time. Herb vinegars are versatile and will keep for several years, becoming more mellow as they age. Use a good wine or cider vinegar.

FREEZING SPRIGS
Freezing is a good way to preserve herbs and is especially suited to those with fine or soft leaves. Place sprigs in a plastic bag, seal, and freeze.

HERB ICE CUBES
Some herbs, such as borage and mint, can be used to flavor drinks. Chop the herbs (leaving decorative flowers whole), place in an ice-cube tray, fill with water, and freeze.

HERBS IN VINEGAR
This vinegar combines the flavors of dill and anise, delicious used in a salad dressing or in a fish dish. Lightly crush the herbs before putting in the bottle. Add the vinegar and allow to steep for at least three weeks.

A Catalog of Herbs

This catalog provides a guide to some of the most popular herbs. Descriptions include suggestions for how plants might be used in the garden, as well as in cooking, with tips on preserving and propagating them. Symbols indicate each herb's preferred growing conditions and hardiness.

Prefers full sun *Prefers partial shade* *Tolerates full shade* *Prefers well-drained soil* *Prefers moist soil* *Prefers wet soil* **Large** *Taller than 4ft/1.2m* **Medium** *2–4ft/60cm–1.2m* **Small** *Up to 2ft/60cm* *Hardiness zone ranges are given as* **Zx–x**

A

Achillea millefolium
Yarrow
A small, mat-forming perennial bearing flattened flowerheads in white, cream, or pale pink in summer. The fernlike gray-green leaves are aromatic when crushed. Deeper pink or red yarrows make attractive border plants. Flowers last well when cut.
Uses Medicinally, it is used to staunch cuts and reduce fever. Contact may irritate skin. Flowers can be dried for decoration.
Cultivation Can be invasive. Divide in autumn or spring; sow seed in spring.
Z3–9

Pink-flowered Yarrow 'Lilac Beauty'

Agastache foeniculum
Anise hyssop
Spikes of blue-purple flowers open from midsummer to early autumn. A medium-sized perennial, it makes an attractive border plant.
Uses The anise-flavored leaves can be used in salads or as a sweetener. Medicinally, the plant is used to treat coughs. Preserve by drying.
Cultivation Needs a sheltered site to survive winters in cold areas. Sow seed in spring, divide in spring, or take cuttings in early summer.
Z6–10

Agrimonia eupatoria
Agrimony
A medium-sized perennial with slender spikes of small, sweet-smelling yellow flowers in summer. Best suited to an informal border or wildflower meadow. Attracts bees.
Uses Dried flowers add a honey scent to potpourri. Medicinally, it is prescribed for mild digestive problems, sore throats, phlegm, and some skin conditions.
Cultivation Sow seed in spring; divide in spring or autumn.
Z6–9

Agrimony

ALLIUM: Chives, garlic, onions

Some alliums are grown for their flowers, others to flavor food. A few are perfect in both roles.

A. schoenoprasum
Chives
Small perennial with round heads of usually pink-purple flowers in early summer. The leaves are tubular and taste mildly of onions.
Uses Use leaves in salads, sauces, and to flavor many cooked dishes. Preserve by freezing or drying.
Cultivation Sow seed in spring; divide in autumn or spring. Easily grown in containers. Lift and pot for indoor winter use (*see p.55*).
Z3–9

A. tuberosum
Garlic/Chinese chives
In late summer, clusters of white flowers are carried above the clumps of strap-shaped, garlic-flavored leaves. A small perennial.

CHIVES

RAMSONS

Uses As chives and in stir-fries and Chinese cooking.
Cultivation As chives.
Z4–8

A. sativum
Garlic
A medium-sized bulbous perennial (if unharvested) with clusters of bell-shaped flowers in summer.
Uses Bulbs are used in cooking worldwide. Medicinally, it helps fight infections, especially colds.
Cultivation Harvest in late summer and early autumn; store bulbs in a cool place. Plant individual cloves for new plants in autumn or late winter.
Z4–9

Other alliums
Onion, *A. cepa*: an essential ingredient for cooking, but also used in dyeing. Z4–9
Ramsons or wild garlic, *A. ursinum*: perennial for lightly shaded wild gardens; can be grown in woodland areas. White flowers open in late spring. **Z4–9**

Aloysia triphylla
Lemon verbena
The leaves of this deciduous, medium-sized to large shrub have a strong lemon aroma. Spikes of tiny white flowers appear in summer.
Uses Fresh leaves can be used to flavor drinks and both sweet and savory dishes. Leaves can also be dried for infusions or potpourris. It is used in aromatherapy.
Cultivation Protect in a greenhouse or conservatory in cold areas in winter. Suitable for growing in containers.
Z8–11

Alpine (wild) strawberry
see Fragaria

Anethum graveolens
Dill
A medium-sized annual with feathery foliage and flattened heads of yellow flowers.
Uses Leaves and seeds are delicious in potato, egg, and seafood dishes. Medicinally, it aids digestion. Freeze or dry leaves to preserve; dry seeds.
Cultivation Sow seed from spring to summer for a continuous supply. Goes to seed quickly in dry soil.
Annual

DILL

ANGELICA

CHERVIL

Angelica archangelica
Angelica
Large, statuesque plant with domed heads of tiny yellow-green flowers in summer. Usually grown as a biennial.
Uses The aromatic leaves can be eaten in salads or infused as a tea; the roots and seeds are added to liqueurs. Crystallized stems are used to decorate confectionery. Medicinal uses include easing bronchial congestion and digestive problems. Stems, leaves, and seeds can be preserved by drying.
Cultivation Sow seed *in situ* as soon as it ripens or in spring. Cutting flowerheads to prevent seeds from forming may prolong the life of the plant and prevents self-seeding.
Z4–9

Anise hyssop *see Agastache*

Anthriscus cerefolium
Chervil
A small, pretty annual with fernlike leaves and tiny white flowers in midsummer. It grows well in a cool site but tends to go to seed in full sun.
Uses The anise-flavored leaves are a traditional ingredient of *fines herbes* in French cooking; they can also be added to potato, egg, or fish dishes. Medicinally, chervil is prescribed to soothe inflamed eyes. Preserve leaves by freezing or drying.
Cultivation For a continuous supply of leaves, sow seed in succession from spring to autumn. Can be grown in a container in light shade.
Annual

Apium graveolens
Wild celery, smallage
An ancestor of the cultivated celery that is grown for the table. Loose heads of tiny, greenish white flowers are carried on medium-sized plants with divided leaves. Can be annual or biennial. Suitable for informal herb gardens.
Uses Seldom used in cooking, although the seeds are sometimes used to flavor salt. Medicinally, it is prescribed to ease indigestion.
Cultivation Sow seed in spring.
Z7–9

Artemisia
Artemisia
Most artemisias have aromatic, divided, silver or gray-green leaves, and many are grown purely for their ornamental effect. Most thrive in sunny sites with poor soil.

A. dracunculus
French tarragon
A large, upright perennial with narrow green leaves that have a mint-anise flavor. The type called Russian tarragon (*A. dracunculus dracunculoides*) is hardier but it has a coarser taste and can be invasive.
Uses Especially good with chicken and egg dishes. Pick leaves before flowering. Preserve by drying or freezing.
Cultivation Protect in cold areas. Take cuttings in late spring or early summer.
Z4–7

Other artemisias
A. abrotanum, southernwood: upright shrub, usually deciduous, with finely cut, aromatic gray-green leaves. Cut back in early spring to keep in shape. **Z6–10**
A. absinthum, absinthe: medium-sized, woody-based perennial, once the bitter element in the liqueur absinthe. Suitable for mixed borders. **Z3–9**
A. ludoviciana, Western mugwort: medium-sized, spreading perennial with silvery leaves. Z4–7

RUSSIAN TARRAGON

Arugula *see Eruca*

BORAGE

B

Basil *see Ocimum*

Bay *see Laurus*

Bee balm *see Monarda*

Borago officinalis
Borage
Medium to large annual, ideal for informal plantings. Blue star-shaped flowers appear in summer. The leaves and flowers taste of cucumber.
Uses Fresh leaves and flowers are added to salads and drinks, such as fruit punches. Flowers can also be candied. Medicinally, borage acts as a mild sedative. Preserve leaves by drying or freezing; flowers can be frozen in ice cubes.
Cultivation Sow seed in spring or autumn. Cut old flowerheads to prevent self-seeding.
☀ ♢ Annual

Buxus
Boxwood
Much used as an edging in formal herb gardens, this slow-growing, evergreen shrub is ideally suited to clipping and is also excellent for topiary. The classic choice for growing as low hedges is small-leaved *B. sempervirens* 'Suffruticosa'; 'Argenteo-variegata' and 'Aureovariegata' are also good for edging, with silver- and gold-edged leaves respectively.
Uses Leaves are toxic if eaten and used only in homeopathy.
Cultivation Clip to shape regularly; will eventually grow into a large shrub if left untrimmed.
☀ ♢ Z5–8

C–D

Calendula officinalis
Pot marigold
A small, brightly colored annual with yellow or orange flowers during cool weather. These also come in cream and tawny shades. Marigolds are perfect for cottage garden-style plantings.
Uses Fresh or dried flowers can be used to give food a tangy flavor and golden color. The leaves can also be added to salads. The flowers can be boiled to make a dye. Medicinally, the plant is soothing and antiseptic and is included in many commercial lotions. Preserve the flowers by drying.
Cultivation Sow seed *in situ* in autumn or spring. Dead-head to prolong flowering and restrict self-seeding.
☀ ♢ Annual

POT MARIGOLD

Carum carvi
Caraway
A small to medium, upright biennial with feathery, aromatic, bright green foliage. The open heads of tiny white flowers are followed by ribbed brown seeds if the summer is sufficiently long and warm.
Uses Young leaves give salads and soups a mild, dill-like flavor. The pungent seeds are much used in eastern European cooking, especially in bread and confectionery. Medicinally, caraway is prescribed to ease digestion.
Cultivation Sow seed *in situ* from late spring to late summer. May self-seed. It can be grown in pots indoors.
☀ ♢ Z5–8

Catmint, catnip *see Nepeta*

CARAWAY

Chamaemelum nobile
Chamomile
The feathery leaves of this small perennial are strongly scented when crushed. White daisy flowers appear in summer. The double-flowered 'Flore Pleno' makes a pretty edging. Low-growing forms are used to make small lawns (not hard-wearing) or seats.
Uses The flowers make a tea that acts as a mild sedative. Medicinally, it is prescribed for bronchial congestion. Preserve flowers by drying.
Cultivation Divide plants in spring or sow seed *in situ*. Choose the nonflowering 'Treneague' for lawns, spacing plants 4in/10cm apart.
☼ ♁ Z4–8

Chervil *see Anthriscus*

Chives *see Allium*

Comfrey *see Symphytum*

Coriandrum sativum
Cilantro, Coriander
An upright, small to medium annual. Lower leaves (cilantro) resemble parsley but become threadlike higher up the plant. Clusters of tiny white flowers are borne from midsummer to autumn, followed by seedheads full of round, pale brown seeds (coriander).
Uses The fresh, tangy leaves are a widely used flavoring, especially in Middle Eastern, Mexican, and Southeast Asian cooking. The seeds are used in numerous dishes including curries and pickles, as well as in spirits such as gin and Chartreuse. Medicinally, seeds are taken for minor digestive problems. Their oil can help relieve painful joints. Preserve leaves by freezing; seeds by drying.
Cultivation Sow *in situ* from spring to early summer. Grow in full sun to produce seeds and in part shade for foliage; otherwise, plants go to seed without forming many leaves.
☼☀ ♁ Annual

CILANTRO

Crocus sativus
Saffron
A small crocus that needs long, hot summers to produce its purple flowers in autumn.
Uses The long orange stigmas in the center of the flower are dried to make saffron, which flavors and adds a rich gold color to Mediterranean dishes such as paella and risotto.
Cultivation Sow seed as soon as it ripens or separate offsets from corms in late spring.
☼ ♁ Z4–8

SAFFRON CROCUS

Curry plant *see Helichrysum*

Dill *see Anethum*

E

Eruca vesicaria* subsp. *sativa
Arugula
A popular salad plant, the leaves of this fast-growing, small to medium annual can be ready to pick a month after sowing.
Uses Leaves add a peppery tang to salads and sauces. Pick young before their flavor coarsens.
Cultivation Sow batches *in situ* from late winter to early summer, and again in late summer. Will self-seed. Can be grown in containers.
☼ ♁ Annual

ARUGULA

Evening primrose *see Oenothera*

F–G

Fennel *see Foeniculum*

Feverfew *see Tanacetum*

Filipendula ulmaria
Meadowsweet
An elegant, medium-sized perennial for damp gardens, growing natively in waterside meadows. The heads of tiny cream flowers have a sweet, marzipan-like scent; the lobed, dark green leaves have a sharper aroma. 'Variegata' has leaves splashed with yellow, fading to cream as the flowers form.
Uses Medicinally, it is prescribed for pain relief and gastric upsets. Once grown as a strewing herb. The dried flowers and leaves are used in potpourris.
Cultivation Divide plants in autumn or spring.
Z3–9

MEADOWSWEET

FENNEL

Foeniculum vulgare
Fennel
A large plant with stems of feathery foliage that add grace and height to any style of garden. Flat heads of tiny yellow flowers are borne in summer. Bronze-colored 'Purpureum' is particularly decorative. Plants can be biennial or perennial.
Uses The anise-flavored leaves and seeds are widely used in cooking, the leaves especially with oily fish. Medicinally, fennel is taken as a breath freshener and to ease digestion. Preserve the leaves by freezing or drying and the seeds by drying.
Cultivation Sow seed in spring. Plants self-seed freely.
Z4–9

Fragaria vesca
Alpine or wild strawberry
A low-growing perennial with small, sweet fruit in summer following the white flowers. Can be grown in pots or in mixed beds or borders. Makes a dainty edging for paths.
Uses The fruit, delicious fresh, can be preserved in jams and syrups. Medicinally, it is mildly diuretic. Leaves and roots are used dried to relieve digestive problems. Harvest leaves in early summer.
Cultivation Sow seed in spring. Enrich soil beforehand with organic matter such as compost. Plants tend to deteriorate and need renewing after a few years.
Z5–9

French tarragon *see Artemisia dracunculus*

Galium odoratum
Sweet woodruff
A small, spreading perennial with starry white flowers in spring and early summer. Good groundcover in shade.
Uses Dried leaves, which smell of new-mown hay, are added to potpourris and pillows. Fresh leaves are also used in *Maitrank*, a German wine punch. Medicinally,

SWEET WOODRUFF

SUNFLOWER

sweet woodruff acts as a mild diuretic and laxative.
Cultivation Divide in spring to make more plants.
☼ ♦ Z3–9

Garlic, garlic chives
see Allium

H

Helianthus annuus
Sunflower
With its huge, golden flowers in summer, this large, fast-growing annual makes a bold plant for an herb garden.
Uses The seeds are delicious raw or roasted and are widely used in baking. They can also be sprouted and added to salads. Medicinally, they are prescribed to relieve coughs and gastric problems. Harvest in autumn.
Cultivation To grow the tallest plants, enrich soil with well-rotted manure or compost prior to sowing. Sow seed *in situ*; delay sowing until late spring to avoid seedlings being killed by frost.
☼ ◊ Annual

Helichrysum italicum
Curry plant
A small to medium-sized shrubby evergreen whose silvery, needlelike leaves have a sweetish curry scent. Small, flattened yellow flowerheads appear from summer to autumn. *H. italicum* 'Nanum' is a dwarf version.
Uses The flowers dry well and can be used in winter arrangements. Dried flowers and leaves can be added to potpourris. The leaves add a mild curry flavor to rice, vegetables, and savory dishes.
Cultivation Cut back in spring to keep plants in good shape, taking out any winter-damaged shoots. Plants are more likely to survive winters in cold areas if drainage is good. Sow seed in autumn or spring.
☼ ◊ Z7–9

DWARF CURRY PLANT (*H. ITALICUM* 'NANUM')

Hypericum perforatum
St. John's wort
In summer, this medium-sized perennial bears star-shaped yellow flowers. Its mid-green leaves have large, translucent dots that contain the oil used in herbal remedies.
Uses Externally, it is used to sooth burns, bruises, sprains and cramps. St. John's wort is also prescribed to treat anxiety and nervous tension.
NB Foliage is harmful if eaten.
Cultivation Sow seed in spring, or make new plants by detaching rooted runners in spring or autumn.
☼ ◊ Z4–8

ST. JOHN'S WORT

WHITE-FLOWERED HYSSOP (*H. OFFICINALIS* F. *ALBUS*)

Hyssopus officinalis
Hyssop
A delightful small, semi-evergreen shrub, perfect for cottage gardens. The spikes of tubular flowers, in varying shades of blue or sometimes pink or white, appear from midsummer to autumn and are attractive to bees.
H. officinalis subsp. *aristatus* is a dwarf hyssop suitable for rock gardens or containers or as a low edging for beds and borders.
Uses The flowerheads and young leaves dry well and can be added to potpourris. The leaves have a rather bitter, sagelike flavor and can be used sparingly with meat, especially game, and in bean and lentil dishes. Hyssop is also a flavoring in liqueurs such as Chartreuse. The oil is soothing when added to a bath. Medicinally, hyssop has a range of uses, but the oil is toxic if taken in quantity, and its use is restricted by law in some countries.
Cultivation Cut back in spring to keep plants shapely. Sow seed in autumn or spring.
☼ ◊ Z3–9

I

Isatis tinctoria
Woad
This large, taprooted biennial or short-lived perennial has long been cultivated for its blue dye, although it may not be the plant reputedly used by ancient Britons to color their skin. It can make an attractive garden plant, with its gray-green leaves and clusters of yellow flowers in summer, followed by black seeds.
Uses Medicinally, used to reduce inflammation and fever, and reputedly has anti-cancer effects. Dye plant.
Cultivation Sow seed in autumn or spring. Self-sown seedlings are best transplanted to a fresh site.
☼ ◊ Z3–8

L

Laurus nobilis
Bay
Native to the Mediterranean, this evergeen large shrub or tree makes a handsome architectural plant for an herb garden, especially if trained as a mop-headed standard. It withstands regular clipping and is suitable for growing in containers. The leaves are a glossy green, and clusters of greenish yellow flowers appear in spring. There is also a selection with golden leaves.
Uses The leaves are much used in cooking, usually dried, and are an essential ingredient of a *bouquet garni.* They can be added to sauces, stews, soups, and even desserts. Dry leaves whole; they keep their flavor for up to a year. Medicinally, bay eases aches caused by sprains, bruises, and rheumatism.
Cultivation Where hardy outdoors, shelter them from cold winter winds, which can brown the leaves. Where not hardy, plants growing in containers must be moved into a greenhouse or conservatory in winter.
☼ ◊ Z8–10

Lavender cotton *see Santolina*

Lemon balm *see Melissa*

Lemon verbena *see Aloysia*

BAY

LAVANDULA: Lavender

Invaluable for the fragrance of their late summer flowers and silver, gray, or green foliage, these small to medium-sized shrubs can be grown in mixed borders, as low hedges, and in pots.

L. angustifolia
Common lavender
Compact, with flowers in mauve, pink, or white. Purple 'Hidcote' is good for hedging and edging.
Uses Dried flowers are used in potpourris, to scent linen, and for winter decoration. The essential oil is used in aromatherapy, perfume and cosmetics, and, medicinally, as an insect repellent and to soothe burns and stings.
Cultivation Trim in early spring to keep in shape, but do not cut into old wood.
☼ ♢ **Z5–8**

Other lavenders
English lavender, *L.* × *intermedia*: rounded shape. **Z5–8**
French lavender, *L. stoechas*: flowers have feathery bracts. **Z8–9**

FRENCH LAVENDER (*L. STOECHAS*)

DWARF WHITE LAVENDER (*L. ANGUSTIFOLIA* 'NANA ALBA')

LOVAGE

Levisticum officinale
Lovage
This vigorous perennial bears flattened clusters of tiny yellow-green flowers in midsummer, followed by crescent-shaped seeds. A large plant, it needs plenty of space. Its bold foliage can make a handsome addition to the flower border.
Uses The leaves smell and taste strongly of yeast and celery and can be used in salads and to flavor soups and other cooked dishes. Young shoots can be eaten raw or steamed. The seeds are used in baking and for flavoring drinks. Preserve the leaves by freezing or drying; seeds by drying. The foliage may irritate skin.
Cultivation Sow seed as soon as it ripens or in spring; divide in spring.
☼ ♢ **Z5–8**

Lovage *see Levisticum*

Lungwort *see Pulmonaria*

M

Marjoram *see Origanum*

Meadowsweet *see Filipendula*

Melissa officinalis
Lemon balm
A bushy, medium-sized perennial with lemon-scented leaves. The young foliage of golden-variegated 'Aurea' is particularly attractive in late spring and early summer.
Uses Fresh leaves give a delicate lemon flavor to salads, white fish dishes, and fruit desserts. Dried, they are used for herb teas and in potpourris.
Cultivation Cut plants back after flowering to produce plenty of fresh foliage. Variegated plants have a tendency to produce shoots that have reverted to plain green. Take these out at the base or they will eventually take over the plant. Divide in autumn or spring, or sow seed in spring; it may be slow to germinate.
☼ ♢ **Z4–9**

MENTHA: Mint

Small- to medium-sized perennials with creeping roots; generally invasive, so best planted in a container sunk in the ground.

M. spicata
Spearmint
The most commonly grown. 'Crispa' has decoratively curled leaves; 'Moroccan' has a good flavor.
Uses Flavors potatoes, mint sauce, and numerous dishes, especially Middle Eastern. Makes a refreshing tea. Medicinally, helps relieve colds. Preserve by drying.
Cultivation All mints can be divided in spring or autumn.
Z4–9

M. × gracilis
Gingermint
Has a sweet scent. Yellow-and-green-leaved 'Variegata' looks attractive and is less invasive.
Uses Add to fruit salad. Z7–9

M. × piperita
Peppermint
Uses Good in drinks; can aid digestion. Z4–9

M. requienii
Corsican mint
Tiny-leaved, creeping plant.
Uses Excellent for planting in paving in shade. Z7–9

GINGER-MINT

***M. suaveolens* 'Variegata'**
Pineapple mint
Leaves are splashed cream.
Uses Add to punches. Z2–9

Monarda
Bee balm
A medium-sized, clump-forming perennial that brings color to the herb garden and attracts bees. The ornamental flowers, mainly pink, purple, or red, appear in summer and autumn. The two main species are *M. didyma* (often called bergamot) and wild bee balm, *M. fistulosa*.
Uses Leaves of *M. didyma* are added to iced drinks and give tea a distinctive aroma. *M. fistulosa* is infused as a tea. Medicinally, bee balm is prescribed to ease digestive disorders. Preserve leaves and flowers by drying.
Cultivation Divide in spring, or sow seed in spring or autumn.
Z4–10

WILD BEE BALM

Myrrhis odorata
Sweet cicely
A large, clump-forming perennial with fernlike leaves and dainty clusters of small white flowers in spring, followed by long seed cases.
Uses The anise-flavored leaves are used to sweeten fruit dishes; the seeds make an interesting ingredient in salads and fruit salads. Preserve leaves by freezing.
Cultivation Sow seed in spring; divide in autumn or spring. Plants will self-seed.
Z3-7

Myrtus communis
Myrtle
An aromatic evergreen shrub with small glossy leaves and fragrant cream flowers, single or double, in late summer. Grows slowly to a large plant.
Uses The leaves flavor pork and poultry dishes. The oil is used in perfumery, and the flowers dry well for potpourri.

DOUBLE-FLOWERED MYRTLE (*M. COMMUNIS* 'FLORE PLENO')

Medicinally, myrtle is used to treat urinary and respiratory problems.
Cultivation Plant out of cold winds, which scorch leaves. Suitable for containers, but in many areas needs to be moved into a greenhouse or conservatory for winter.
☼ ◊ Z9–10

N-O

Nasturtium *see Tropaeolum*

Nepeta cataria
Catnip
Although there are several decorative, blue-flowered nepetas (catmint), such as *N.* × *faassenii*, this is the plant with magnetic appeal for cats. A medium-sized perennial, it has grayish leaves and white flowers in summer.
Uses Dried leaves can be used to flavor meat, infused to relieve colds, or put in mouse-shaped sachets for cats' toys.
Cultivation Divide in autumn or spring; sow seed in autumn.
☼ ◊ Z4–9

OCIMUM: Basil

Powerfully aromatic herb, much used in cooking, especially in Mediterranean and Southeast Asian cuisines. Generally grown as annuals, there are several different types; flavors vary among them.

O. basilicum
Sweet basil
Small, bushy plant with spikes of white flowers from summer to autumn. There are many to choose from: 'Mini Purpurascens Wellsweep' is particularly compact, with purple leaves and pink flowers; 'Green Ruffles' has huge, crinkled leaves, and 'Horapha' (Thai basil) has a slight anise flavor. *O. basilicum* var. *minimum*, bush or Greek basil, is a small-leaved, compact plant that can be used as an edging to beds.
Uses Fresh leaves are delicious with tomatoes, pasta, and in soup and are used in Thai curries. Best preserved by freezing. Basil is used in aromatherapy.
Cultivation Needs sun and a sheltered site. Good results are achieved from growing in pots under glass or on a sunny windowsill or patio. Pinch out shoot tips to make plants bushy. Flavor coarsens once flowers form. Sow seed in late spring.
☼ ◊ Annual

SWEET BASIL 'MINI PURPURASCENS WELLSWEEP'

Other basils
Holy basil, *O. tenuiflorum*: downy leaves, which also taste slightly of mint. Used in Thai cooking.

SWEET BASIL

SWEET BASIL 'GREEN RUFFLES'

Oenothera biennis
Evening primrose
A large, upright annual or biennial, ideal for informal herb gardens, especially if allowed to self-seed. Spikes of fragrant, pale yellow, bowl-shaped flowers open on summer evenings. They turn a darker gold as they age and are followed by downy pods containing tiny round seeds; the oil from these is rich in gamma-linoleic acid.
Uses The therapeutic qualities of the acid were only recently discovered; it is added to creams for dry skin and combined with other ingredients to relieve menstrual problems.
Cultivation Sow seed *in situ* from late summer to autumn. Can be grown in quite poor, stony ground.
☼ ◊ **Z5–8**

Onion *see Allium*

ORIGANUM: Marjoram

Compact marjorams are ideal in pots and as edging; others suit mixed plantings. Some have variegated or gold foliage. White or lilac flowers appear in summer.

O. majorana
Sweet marjoram
Medium-sized annual.
Uses Good in tomato and onion dishes, especially of Mediterranean origin. Leaves and flowers can be used to make tea. Preserve by drying.
Cultivation Sow seed in autumn or spring.
☼ ◊ Annual

O. onites
Pot marjoram
Small, leafy perennial.
Uses Adds a more pungent flavor to food than sweet marjoram.
Cultivation As above, or take cuttings in late spring. **Z8–10**

O. vulgare
Wild marjoram, oregano
Small perennial. Gold-leaved 'Aureum' is best in light shade; 'Compactum' makes a neat edging.
Uses Flavors food (as for sweet marjoram).
Cultivation As above. **Z6–9**

POT MARJORAM

WILD MARJORAM

PELARGONIUM 'FAIR ELLEN'

P

Parsley *see Petroselinum crispum*

Pelargonium
Scented geraniums
Grown for their aromatic leaves, scented geraniums look very different from the bold-flowered geraniums used as summer bedding. Most have small flowers in mauve, pink, purple, or white and make small, bushy, tender perennials. Leaf shape and size varies, as does perfume, ranging from peppermint to rose and spice to eucalyptus. 'Fair Ellen' (*above*) has balsam-scented leaves.
Uses Dried leaves are excellent in potpourris. They can also be infused to flavor desserts and cakes; *P. crispum* 'Variegatum' adds a lemon taste. The essential oil, particularly of rose-scented 'Graveolens', is much used in perfumery and aromatherapy.
Cultivation In most areas, best grown in pots that can easily be moved indoors in

ITALIAN PARSLEY

winter. Cut back in spring to prevent plants from becoming leggy. Take cuttings in late spring or early summer.
Min 35°F/2°C

Petroselinum crispum
Parsley
This small, clump-forming biennial is one of the most widely used culinary herbs. Curly *P. crispum* has tightly crinkled leaves; *P. crispum* var. *neapolitanum*, often called Italian or French parsley, has flatter leaves.

CURLY-LEAVED PARSLEY

Uses Curly parsley has a clean taste and is best used fresh as a garnish or in salads. Flat-leaved parsley is stronger and is suited to cooked dishes. The flavor coarsens once flowers form. Preserve leaves by freezing.
Cultivation Sow seed in succession between spring and late summer. It can be sparse and slow to germinate.
Z6–9

Pot marigold *see Calendula*

Pulmonaria officinalis
Lungwort
A small, evergreen perennial with large, silver-spotted leaves, good for border edges and in wild or woodland settings where it can spread. The funnel-shaped flowers age gradually from pink to gray-blue.
Uses Medicinally, lungwort was once used to treat bronchial diseases and is still prescribed as an expectorant.
Cultivation Cut back after flowering to encourage fresh foliage. Divide in autumn or after flowering.
Z3–9

R–S

Rosmarinus
Rosemary
This large, bushy, evergreen shrub looks very ornamental planted in mixed borders or in pots. Blue flowers (sometimes pink or white) open in spring. Some grow upright; choose low, spreading types for trailing over low walls or banks.
Uses The needlelike, aromatic

ROSEMARY 'PRIMLEY BLUE'

leaves are good for flavoring meat, especially lamb and pork, and oils and vinegars. Rosemary is also used in bath preparations and shampoos. Preserve leaves and sprigs by drying; they keep their flavor well.
Cultivation Cut back after flowering to prevent plants from becoming lanky. Avoid cutting into old wood. Plants can survive low temperatures better if drainage is good. Sow seed in spring.
Z8–10

ROSEMARY

French Sorrel

Rumex
Sorrel
Medium-sized perennials grown for their acidic-tasting leaves. *R. acetosa*, common sorrel, is most widely used. The small, mat-forming *R. scutatus*, French or buckler-leaf sorrel, has a similar taste. Many relatives, including dock, are invasive weeds.
Uses Use leaves sparingly in salads, soups, and sauces for fish. Harvest the leaves before plants form their spikes of tiny green flowers.
Cultivation Sow seed in spring; divide in autumn or spring.
☼ ♢ Z4–8

Ruta graveolens
Rue
This small- to medium-sized, pungent-smelling shrub has attractive, finely divided, blue-green leaves. Yellow flowers appear in summer. There is a variegated rue with leaves splashed with cream.
Uses In homeopathy, rue is used as a remedy for sprains, bruising, eye problems, and indigestion. Bitter-tasting, it has no culinary uses except as a flavoring for the Italian spirit *grappa*. Avoid contact with skin: in bright sunlight, it can cause bad blistering.

Rue

Cultivation Will tolerate hot, dry sites. Sow seed in spring.
☼ ♢ Z4–8

St. John's wort *see Hypericum*

Saffron *see Crocus*

SALVIA: Sage

A wide-ranging genus, most salvias are purely decorative, although the culinary sages also make extremely attractive garden plants.
S. officinalis
Common sage
The most widely cultivated for culinary use. A medium-sized shrubby perennial, with either gray-green or colored foliage (*see right*).
Uses Leaves are mainly used to flavor meat. Preserve by drying.
Cultivation Cut back in spring to keep in shape. Sow seed in spring; take cuttings in spring or summer.
☼ ♢ Z5–9

Other species
Pineapple sage, *S. elegans* 'Scarlet Pineapple': large, scarlet-flowered. Leaves used in punches. Min 35°F/2°C.

Clary sage, *S. sclarea*: open spires of cream, pink, or lilac flowers are suitable for dried decorations. A medium-sized biennial or perennial. Z4–9

Golden Sage ('Icterina')

Purple Sage (Purpurascens Group)

Sanguisorba minor
Salad burnet
A small, clump-forming perennial with attractively divided leaves and egg-shaped heads of tiny rust-colored flowers in summer.
Uses The leaves have a cucumber scent when crushed and can be added fresh to salads and summer drinks. Harvest before flowers open.
Cultivation Sow seed or divide in autumn or spring.
☼ ◊ Z5–8

Santolina chamaecyparissus
Lavender cotton
Tiny, yellow, buttonlike flowers decorate this small, round, evergreen shrub from midsummer. These are held on long stems above the feathery gray-white leaves. Lavender cotton is often used as an edging in knot gardens.
Uses Dried leaves and flowers can be added to potpourris, or kept in closets to repel moths. Santolina was once used for skin irritations and against intestinal parasites; it is rarely used for medicinal purposes today. Preserve leaves and flowers by drying.
Cultivation Sow in autumn or spring, or take cuttings in early summer.
☼ ◊ Z6–8

Satureja
Savory
There are several types of savory. Summer savory, *S. hortensis*, is a small, bushy annual with narrow leaves and white or lilac flowers. Winter savory, *S. montana*, Z5–8, is a small, shrubby perennial with whitish pink flowers. It can be used to edge beds or grown at the front of

CREEPING SAVORY

a border. The perennial thyme-leaved savory, *S. thymbra*, Z8–9, is also small and shrubby, with pink flowers. Used as an edging. Creeping savory, *S. spicigera*, Z7–8, is a prostrate plant that looks good between paving stones.
Uses The leaves, especially of summer and winter savory, add a spicy, peppery flavor to meat and legumes. Preserve by drying.
Cultivation Give plants a light trim in spring. Sow seed in autumn or spring.
☼ ◊ Hardiness varies

WINTER SAVORY

Scented geranium *see Pelargonium*

Sorrel *see Rumex*

Sunflower *see Helianthus*

Sweet cicely *see Myrrhis*

Sweet woodruff *see Galium*

Symphytum
Comfrey
This large, vigorous perennial has coarse, hairy leaves and bears bell-like pink, lilac, violet, or pale yellow flowers in late spring and summer. Can be used as a groundcover. Variegated comfrey will brighten shady corners.
Uses Comfrey leaves have a long history of use (fresh or dried) in poultices for bruises, sprains, and abrasions. Taking internally is not recommended; it contains alkaloids that, in large amounts, can cause liver damage. Contact with foliage may irritate skin.
Cultivation Sow seed in autumn or spring; divide in spring. Can be invasive.
☼ ♦ Z4–9

VARIEGATED COMFREY (*S. × UPLANDICUM* 'VARIEGATUM')

TANSY 'ISLA GOLD'

FEVERFEW

T

Tanacetum
Feverfew, tansy, alecost
With their daisylike flowers and deeply cut leaves, it is worth including at least one of these perennials in the herb garden. Feverfew, *T. parthenium*, has forms excellent for edging borders. Single or double flowers, white with a golden eye, appear above aromatic foliage in summer. 'Aureum' has golden leaves. Although short-lived, plants readily self-seed. Tansy, *T. vulgare*, is medium-sized, spreading, and vigorous, its upright stems topped with heads of bright yellow, buttonlike flowers in late summer. Alecost, *T. balsamita*, another medium-sized plant, is less decorative. Small white daisy flowers appear in late summer and autumn above its mint-scented leaves.
Uses All can be added to pot-pourris. Medicinally, feverfew soothes insect bites and bruises but can irritate skin. Traditionally, it was used to relieve colds and fevers, but in recent clinical trials has been found to be successful in alleviating migraines. Fresh leaves may cause mouth ulcers if taken in quantity. Tansy leaves give a bitter, rosemary-like flavor to meat dishes and omelettes. Branches can be dried whole and used in cabinets to repel insects. Tansy oil is toxic, and use of the herb is legally restricted in some countries. Alecost, once used to flavor beer, can be used sparingly in meat and vegetable dishes. Preserve leaves by drying.
Cultivation Sow seed in late winter or early spring, take cuttings in early summer, or divide in spring or autumn. Feverfew and tansy can be invasive.
☼☀ ◊ **Z4–9** (all of the above)

Tarragon *see Artemisia*

Teucrium chamaedrys
Wall germander
This small, spreading perennial bears purple-pink flowers from summer to autumn. Evergreen leaves are small, with wavy edges. It makes a pretty edging for borders.
Uses Leaves are used to flavor liqueurs and vermouth. Medicinally, it is used for digestive disorders and as an appetite stimulant. It can cause liver damage and is banned in some countries. Preserve leaves by drying.
Cultivation Divide in autumn; sow seed in autumn or spring.
☼ ◊ **Z5–9**

Tropaeolum majus
Nasturtium
An annual that can be small and bushy, or trail or climb. Funnel-shaped flowers in

WALL GERMANDER

THYMUS: Thyme

Thymes, all perennials, tend to make very small, shrubby plants or creeping mats of aromatic foliage. They can be grown in cracks in paving and steps to cover banks, in containers, and in rock gardens and mixed borders and beds. Leaves can be gold or variegated silver or yellow. White, pink, or purple flowers in summer attract bees.

T. serpyllum
Creeping or wild thyme
Mat-forming plant that can withstand being walked on.
Uses Excellent in paving.
Cultivation Sow seed in spring, *in situ* if necessary.
☼ ◊ Z4–8

CREEPING THYME 'RUSSETINGS'

LEMON THYME

T. vulgaris
Common/garden thyme
Mound-forming, shrubby plant. 'Silver Posie' has silver-variegated leaves.
Uses Flavors meat, poultry, and game. Thyme oil is a powerful antiseptic. Preserve leaves by drying.
Cultivation Trim plants in spring, removing dead stems. Sow seed in spring. **Z5–8**

Other thymes
Lemon thyme, *T.* × *citriodorus*: small and bushy with lemon fragrance. **Z5–9** 'Aurea' has golden leaves. Caraway thyme, *T. herba-barona*: creeping plant with caraway scent. **Z6–8**

V–Z

Verbena officinalis
Vervain
A medium-sized, upright perennial with crinkled leaves and long, thin spikes of lilac or mauve flowers from mid- to late summer. Its rather straggly growth needs to be offset by placing it among large-leaved herbs for textural contrast.
Uses Vervain is taken for nervous disorders and for minor injuries and skin problems. It tastes extremely bitter and has no culinary use. Preserve leaves by drying.
Cultivation Pinch out growing tips to encourage stems to branch. Sow seed in autumn or spring, or divide plants in spring.
☼ ◊ Z4–8

Wall germander *see Teucrium*

Wild celery *see Apium*

Woad *see Isatis*

Wormwood *see Artemisia*

Yarrow *see Achillea*

vivid shades of red and yellow are borne from early summer to midautumn. The leaves of 'Empress of India' (*right*) are an attractive blue-green; those of 'Alaska' are splashed cream.
Uses Leaves and flowers add a peppery, cresslike flavor to salads, while the young, round seedpods are often pickled in vinegar and used like capers.
Cultivation Sow seed *in situ* or in trays in spring.
☼ ◊ Annual

NASTURTIUM 'EMPRESS OF INDIA'

INDEX

Page numbers in ***italics*** indicate illustrations.

ACKNOWLEDGMENTS

Picture Research Mollie Gillard

Special Photography Peter Anderson

Illustrations Gill Tomblin

Additional illustrations Karen Cochrane

Index Hilary Bird

DK Publishing would like to thank:
All staff at the RHS, in particular Susanne Mitchell and Barbara Haynes, at Vincent Square; Frank Hardy and Paul Bearcroft, at Pershore and Hindlip College, Worcestershire, for advice and technical assistance; Candida Frith-Macdonald for editorial assistance; Sarah Cleverdon for help with planting designs; Rosemary Titterington, at Iden Croft Herbs, for advice and assistance; Stanley Tools Ltd.

American Horticultural Society
Visit AHS at **www.ahs.org** or call them at 1-800-777-7931 ext 10. Membership benefits include *The American Gardener* magazine, free admission to flower shows, the free seed exchange, book services, and the Gardener's Information Service.

Photography
The publisher would also like to thank the following for their kind permission to reproduce their photographs:
(key: t=top, b=below, l=left, r=right)

AKG London: Bibliothèque Nationale, Paris 8tr
Bridgeman Art Library, London/New York: A Garden, by Johan Walter, French, Florisège de Nassau-Idstein (1660), Bibliothèque Nationale, Paris 8b
Eric Crichton Photos: 22b
E. T. Archive: British Museum 7br
Garden Picture Library: Jerry Pavia 40; John Glover front cover c, 34; Juliette Wade 6
Garden Matters: 10cr
Jerry Harpur: RHS Chelsea designer: Elizabeth Banks/Daily Telegraph 5bc, 27br; designer Simon Hopkinson/Iden Croft, Kent 12br
John Heseltine Archive: 2
Andrew Lawson: 15tl
Photos Horticultural: 11t; Michael and Lois Warren 9b, 12b
Harry Smith Collection: 28
Steven Wooster: Chelsea Flower Show 5bl